Better Homes and Gardens®

WOOD®
CARVING TECHNIQUES
AND PROJECTS YOU CAN MAKE

WE CARE!

All of us at Meredith® Books are dedicated to giving you the
information and ideas you need to create beautiful and useful
woodworking projects. We guarantee your satisfaction with this
book for as long as you own it. We also welcome your comments
and suggestions. Please write us at Meredith® Books, RW 240,
1716 Locust St., Des Moines, IA 50309-3400.

A **WOOD** BOOK
Published by Meredith Books

MEREDITH BOOKS
President, Book Group: Joseph J. Ward
Vice President and Editorial Director: Elizabeth P. Rice
Executive Editor: Connie Schrader
Art Director: Ernest Shelton
Prepress Production Manager: Randall Yontz

WOOD MAGAZINE
President, Magazine Group: William T. Kerr
Editor: Larry Clayton

CARVING TECHNIQUES AND PROJECTS YOU CAN MAKE
Produced by Roundtable Press, Inc.
Directors: Susan E. Meyer, Marsha Melnick
Senior Editor: Marisa Bulzone
Managing Editor: Ross L. Horowitz
Graphic Designer: Leah Lococo
Design Assistant: Leslie Goldman
Art Assistant: Marianna Canelo Francis
Proofreader: Amy Handy

For Meredith Books
Editorial Project Manager/Associate Art Director: Tom Wegner
Contributing How-To Editors: Marlen Kemmet, Charles E. Sommers
Contributing Techniques Editor: Bill Krier
Contributing Tool Editor: Larry Johnston
Contributing Outline Editor: David A. Kirchner

Special thanks to Khristy Benoit

Meredith Corporation Corporate Officers:
Chairman of the Executive Committee: E. T. Meredith III
Chairman of the Board, President and Chief Executive Officer:
   Jack D. Rehm
Group Presidents: Joseph J. Ward, Books; William T. Kerr, Magazines;
   Philip A. Jones, Broadcasting; Allen L. Sabbag, Real Estate
Vice Presidents: Leo R. Armatis, Corporate Relations;
   Thomas G. Fisher, General Counsel and Secretary;
   Larry D. Hartsook, Finance; Michael A. Sell, Treasurer;
   Kathleen J. Zehr, Controller and Assistant Secretary

On the front cover: Here's Otto the Otter, pages 64–67
On the back cover: Craft a California Whale, page 87;
   Step-By-Step Relief Carving, pages 33–37; Carve a Colorful
   Feather Pin, pages 42–45;

CARVING TOOLS AND MATERIALS

It starts with a knife and a block of wood—and a desire to while away the hours with the most personal kind of woodworking. In this section, we'll tell you how to choose, buy, and even sharpen a basic set of woodcarving tools; describe the best woods for carving; and offer tips for great results.

A Beginner's Guide to Basic Woodcarving Tools

A sharp jackknife and a nice chunk of pine will get you whittling. Woodcarvers, though, use a few more specialized tools, which don't have to cost a lot of money. With the basic set described in this article, you can try your hand at woodcarving, then add more tools later.

Among carvers, whittling means paring away wood from a one-piece, hand-held object with a single tool, usually a knife. With the right kind of knife, you can whittle away a whole bunch of carvings. But you'll find it easier, and less limiting, if you add some specialized tools.

Before we go to these other tools, however, let's look at the all-around favorite carving knife.

A knife that slices, chips, and shaves

Often called a bench knife or a German-style knife, the carving knife shown *below* fits the hand and its blade won't slam shut on your fingers.

A blade length of 1½" handles most carving cuts—a longer blade bends more easily and becomes harder to control. Blades come in either high-carbon or stainless steel—you'll find that high-carbon steel holds an edge longer while stainless needs frequent resharpening. Even though high-carbon steel tends to rust, it's a better choice.

A German-style knife—its short blade and large handle are ideal.

Handles on this type of knife are normally large enough to ease you through several hours of carving.

Prices for a serviceable knife start at $5 through a carving tool supplier, but you can spend $20 or more for a handmade beauty created by a specialty knifemaker.

X-acto knives make good carving tools, too. For their low cost, they feature sharp, surgical steel blades that you discard when dull. Their handles discourage prolonged carving sessions, but for the price they represent a bargain. This type of knife, and others patterned after it, also come in sets that include an assortment of blades.

Gouges remove wood fast

Gouges do woodcarving's "heavy" work. They cut away wood faster than a knife when roughing out a figure or other carving. Fitted into a wooden handle, the metal shafts of most gouges have a curved cutting edge at the end, which tends to scoop out wood rather than split it. Note the curvature of the cutting edge in the illustration *below*.

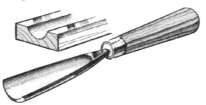

Gouges have curved cutting edges and either straight or angled shanks.

Woodcarving gouges, available in hundreds of shapes and sizes, vary not only in the width of their blades, but also in their curvature or *sweep*. Manufacturers number them accordingly, as depicted in the drawing: *higher numbered gouges indicate a more rounded curvature and therefore a deeper cut.* A No. 1, for example, would be flat and chisel-like. A No. 11 forms approximately a half-circle. The width of their cutting edge, or size, is stated in either inches or millimeters. In addition, the blade will be either straight or curved.

For general use in cutting away wood quickly, a No. 3 or No. 4 straight gouge, ⅜" to ½" wide, works perfectly.

Forged, tempered steel makes the best gouges—less expensive ones are cast. You can detect cast steel by its heaviness and occasional tiny surface pits. Quality handles, normally of hardwood, can be octagonally shaped to prevent rolling in the hand. For long-lasting, well-made gouges, expect to pay from $10 to $15.

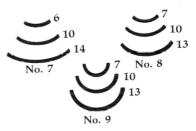

Gouges assigned higher numbers have more sweep to their cutting edge. Numbers to *right* show width in millimeters.

Parting tools carve details

Parting, or V-tools, give you the ability to carve outlines, lettering, sharply defined grooves, and detailing such as hair on an animal or human figure.

Like gouges, parting tools come in a variety of widths and have either curved or straight blade shanks. The V-shaped cutting edge can be specified from 45° to 90° of radius, or spread, as illustrated *below*.

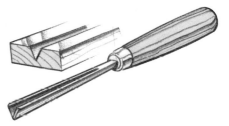

Parting tools vary by width and degree of their V-angle.

continued

A BEGINNER'S GUIDE TO BASIC WOODCARVING TOOLS
continued

For detailing, a parting tool ⅛" wide with a 60° radius works well. A good one, made of forged steel, costs about $10 or less and should last for years of continuous use.

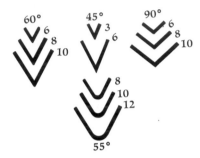

Numbers to *right* are widths in millimeters. Degree numbers indicate depth and incline of cut.

Selecting your carving tools

Keep in mind what you want to carve when you buy tools. For hand-held, three-dimensional pieces such as figures, gouges and parting tools shouldn't be more than 6" long, including the handle. Often called "palm gouges," these fit nicely into the hand.

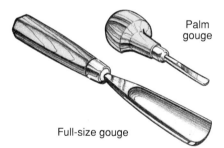

Palm gouge

Full-size gouge

For larger carving projects—those that must be clamped down or held in a vise—you'll need full-size gouges and parting tools that have longer handles and shanks. These larger carving tools can withstand the impact of the carving mallet, often used in wood sculpting, whereas the smaller versions cannot.

Carving tools, as you'll discover when you begin shopping, come in gleaming sets of six to 12 tools titled "professional," "intermediate," or starter, with prices from $25

Five tips on buying carving tools

While interviewing the experts for the carving-tool article that begins *opposite*, we discovered several recurring themes. Keep these pointers in mind. They can save you time and money.

•Buy from a reputable source with a return policy

You can mail-order carving tools from many sources. Why is a return policy important? It's not unusual to order a tool through the mail, only to find out that it's not what you had in mind.

•Buy individual tools rather than sets

You can save a buck or two by buying carving tools in sets, but you usually wind up with a few tools you rarely will use. Buy your tools one at a time, as you need them, and you'll come out dollars ahead in the long run.

•Try tools before buying

If you can sample a carving tool at a store, carving competition, friend's shop, or woodworking show, do it. You'll never know if the tool feels right and cuts as needed until you put the instrument in your hand.

•Check for hairline cracks in the steel

The forging process creates stresses in steel that can lead to tiny cracks, especially near cutting edges. If you spot any cracks—no matter how small—return the tool to the seller immediately.

•Most carving tools do not come presharpened

A few brands, such as Swiss-made and Hirsch/Two Cherries, come presharpened from the factory. But, most brands have factory-ground edges that require honing before you can use them.

---

to more than $200. Avoid the temptation to buy a set. Instead, select your tools individually, then add to them as the need for more specialized ones arise.

For quality tools, you'll pay more, but the difference in cutting efficiency, durability, and comfort makes their initial cost worthwhile. Choose well-balanced tools with good steel—knives with high-carbon blades and forged gouges and parting tools—that feel comfortable in your hand. If you do your shopping by mail, you'll have to rely on the company's reputation and the catalog description to ensure quality. A money-back guarantee also helps to combat dissatisfaction.

Taking care of your tools

Even if you have only a few carving tools, taking care of them pays

off. Well-cared-for carving tools not only last longer, but they're always ready when you get the urge to carve. What could stifle your creativity more than having to hone a knife edge before it can bite into the wood?

"Care" applies to three concerns—sharpening, cleaning, and storage. Sharpening, a lengthy topic, is covered on *page 13*. But here are some pointers about the other two categories:

Cleaning: Every month or so, wipe knife blades and gouges with a rag moistened in light machine oil to prevent rust. Handles can be preserved with linseed oil.

Storage: Keep knives and gouges hanging separately behind your workbench. For even more protection, keep them rolled in a soft cloth, pouch-fashion, in a tool drawer.

HOW TO SHOP SMART FOR CARVING TOOLS

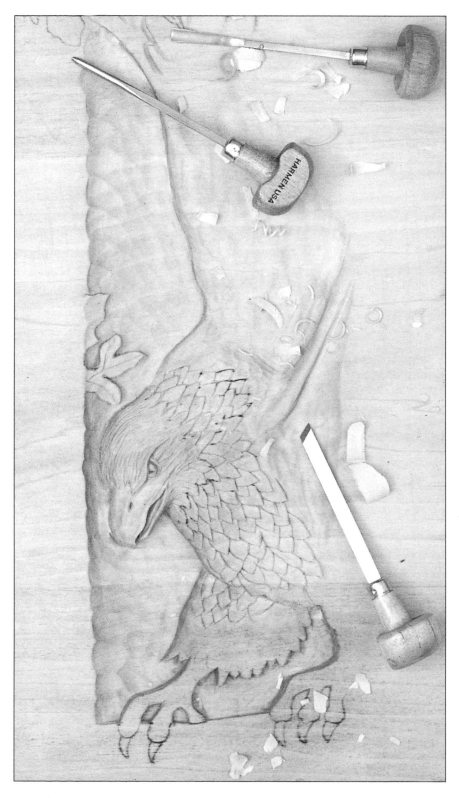

Those of you who have shopped for carving tools know firsthand what a hit-and-miss affair it can be. The instant you make a trial cut with your new purchase, you very well may realize you laid money down for the wrong tool. But armed with the right information, this doesn't need to happen.

Because most of us tend to gravitate toward one style of carving, be it human figures, relief, wildlife, or chip carving (see the explanation of these styles that follows), we asked an expert in each of these fields to tell us about his or her favorite tools. All of them volunteered eagerly to pass along their best tidbits of buying wisdom.

As you'll soon discover, finding the tools that suit your style and pocketbook requires only that you follow a few basic guidelines, mixed in with some sound advice and your own common sense.

First a refresher course
Before we introduce you to our esteemed carvers, we'd like to give you a carving-tool refresher course (see the chart on *pages 9–10*). As you look at the traditional carving tools, remember these two points:
• Except for the bench knife, these tools come mounted in one of the three illustrated handle styles: palm, elongated, or interchangeable. The palm-handle tools have an overall length of 4½–5", whereas the elongated handle tools measure 9½–11" long, including 3½–4"-long blades. You can buy elongated handle carving tools in a far greater array of sizes and styles than palm-handle versions. Interchangeable handles are about 4" long and come in several shapes.

continued

HOW TO SHOP SMART FOR CARVING TOOLS
continued

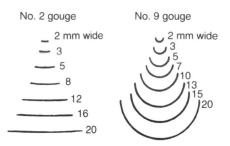

No. 2 gouge

2 mm wide
3
5
8
12
16
20

No. 9 gouge

2 mm wide
3
5
7
10
13
15
20

• The cutting edges of these tools come in various widths (measured in millimeters or inches) and curvatures (known as sweep). As shown in the drawings *above,* carving tools are numbered like golf clubs with a No. 2 gouge having a shallow sweep, and a No. 9 gouge having a good deal of sweep. Gouges numbered between 2 and 9 have degrees of sweep between these two extremes.

Note: *See the article on* page 5 *for more buying pointers.*

Four woodcarving pros speak out

Now that we've given you some general background, select the carver on the next five pages most suited to your style and read on to get the low-down on your favorite type of carving.

Our four pros specialize in these areas: relief, chip, wildlife, and figure carving. Most beginners will have their greatest success in relief and chip carving, both of which require you to carve a flat piece of stock.

Human figure carvings can be as small as your thumb, or larger than life-size, but we advise you to start with smaller subjects in easy-to-carve and less-expensive woods (such as basswood or butternut). Most figure carvers we've run across still rely on traditional carving tools. On the other hand, wildlife carvers generally shape their ducks, fish, and other game with power rotary tools.

Wayne Barton: Chip carver extraordinaire

Few carvers pursue their craft with the passion that Wayne Barton pours into chip carving. He's generally recognized as one of the foremost experts in his field, and it's easy to see why. When he's not operating the Alpine School of Woodcarving in suburban Chicago, he's probably making one of his three or four annual treks to Switzerland to lead tour groups and teach chip carving. Or, he's holding a chip-carving seminar at a woodworking show somewhere in the United States.

Wherever he may be, Wayne quickly points out the merits of chip carving. As he told us: "Compared to other forms of carving, chip carving is more technique than art. Once you know the technique, you can find quick success in this craft. And, it's very economical. You need only two knives: a cutting knife and a stab knife [*above right*] That's it.

Chip carvers need only two tools for all of their work: a cutting knife *(top)* and stab knife.

"The cutting knife is your primary tool, and it does all the chip removal. You use the stab knife mostly for decorative touches. It cuts and spreads the wood fibers to make a wedge-shaped mark, but it doesn't remove the wood," he explained.

Since many carving catalogs show ten or more different chip-carving knives, we asked Wayne how he gets by with just two. "All those knives shown in catalogs were developed for other forms of carving, and somebody decided to sell them as chip-carving knives, but they have no use in chip carving," he told us.

Wayne uses only chip-carving knives made by Klotzli in Switzerland. In fact, you can order his two-piece set from many woodworking catalogs or from the Alpine School of Woodcarving, 225 Vine Avenue, Park Ridge, IL 60068.

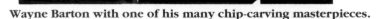

Wayne Barton with one of his many chip-carving masterpieces.

Cathy Blackwood: Relief carver who knows beginners' needs

When we first contacted Cathy about this story, she was rushing out the door of her Soldier, Kansas, home on her way to teach a carving seminar. "Most of the carvers I work with are beginners, so I have a pretty good feel for what they need," she said

to us. When we next talked to her, she had a little more time and told us which tools an aspiring relief carver needs to get a good start.

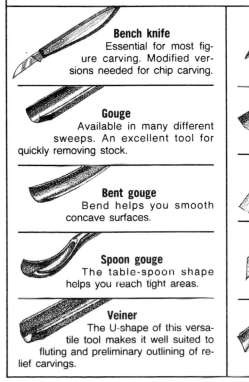

Cathy Blackwood especially likes doing relief carvings of outdoor scenes.

"I like palm-handle tools because their smaller size gives me greater control. Fortunately, I started with two good brands of tools—Harmen and Dastra—and I've always been happy with them. These tools hold an edge well, and only require an occasional honing." Cathy buys her tools from Laughlin Woodcarving Supply in Harrison, Arkansas (see *page 12* for the phone number).

Cathy feels that beginners should start with shallow relief carvings and use these tools:

• Harmen ¼" long-bent V-parting tool for outlining and cleanup.
• Harmen ½" No. 7 gouge for wood removal and shaping.
• Harmen ½" No. 3 gouge for rounding edges, shaping and smoothing unwanted gouge marks.
• Harmen 117 gouge (about ⁵⁄₃₂" wide), a miniature tool for details.
• Dastra 203 2mm spoon chisel for hard-to-reach areas.
• Stanley No. 28-109 retractable knife (see photo *page 10, top left*) for cutting, shaping, and cleaning. "For beginners, I prefer the Stanley retractable model over a bench knife because the blades are flexible and disposable.

AT-A-GLANCE GUIDE TO CARVING TOOLS

Traditional Carving

Bench knife
Essential for most figure carving. Modified versions needed for chip carving.

Gouge
Available in many different sweeps. An excellent tool for quickly removing stock.

Bent gouge
Bend helps you smooth concave surfaces.

Spoon gouge
The table-spoon shape helps you reach tight areas.

Veiner
The U-shape of this versatile tool makes it well suited to fluting and preliminary outlining of relief carvings.

Back-bent gouge
A specialized tool for cleaning out the underside of a cut where top clearance is limited.

Fishtail gouge
Good for cleaning out corners and undercutting.

Chisel
Helps you flatten or round-over a surface.

Skew chisel
Primarily used for rounding-over surfaces. Point helps you remove material from tight areas.

V-parting tool
A handy tool for making outlining cuts and textured lines such as hair or veins.

Bent or spoon-shaped V-parting tool
Fulfills same purpose as a V-parting tool, but shape helps you get cutting edge into tight spots.

Long-bent V-parting tool
The long bend helps you make cuts on concave surfaces.

Elongated handle
Equally useful for carving with just your hands or with hands and mallet.

Palm handle
Some people prefer the feel of a handle they can hold in their palm. Cannot be used with a mallet.

Handle for interchangeable blades
Changing blades requires a few seconds. Made by the Warren Tool Co.

HOW TO SHOP SMART
FOR CARVING TOOLS
continued

Beginning carvers can avoid sharpening chores by using the Stanley retractable knife.

"For the carver ready to take on deeper relief carvings, and those with more fine detail, I suggest making an investment in a Harmen ¼" No. 3 special-design gouge, Harmen 117R miniature V-parting tool, and Dastra 205 4mm gouge."

Rick Beyer: Wildlife specialist

Like most wildlife carvers, Rick Beyer of Racine, Wisconsin, devotes his time to power carving. "It kicks up a little dust, but a power carver helps me work much faster than I could with traditional tools, and with greater control," Rick told us.

Even if you're just getting started in power carving, Rick suggests you start with a flexible-shaft power carver rather than a hand-held motorized tool. "You simply can't do detail work with hand-held tools because they're too awkward and cause too much hand fatigue. For example, details such as bird feathers require that you get your hand in a rhythm,

Rick Beyer specializes in fish carved from black cherry.

and you can only do that with the smaller and lighter handpiece of a flex-shaft machine."

Rick prefers using structured-tooth, tungsten-carbide cutters for shaping, and ruby cutters for smoothing and fine details. "These bits cost more than high-speed steel cutters, or abrasive stones, but give you a lot more control and last much longer."

If you're a rookie to power carving, Rick suggests you start with the less-expensive ⅛"-shaft tools. "Don't make the move to ¼"-shaft and larger tools until you get really serious," he advises.

Rick cites these bits as the ones he uses most often:

• A teardrop-shaped ruby cutter that's about ¼" wide at its broadest

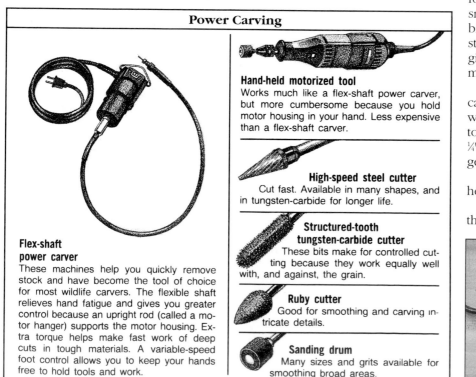

Power Carving

Flex-shaft power carver
These machines help you quickly remove stock and have become the tool of choice for most wildlife carvers. The flexible shaft relieves hand fatigue and gives you greater control because an upright rod (called a motor hanger) supports the motor housing. Extra torque helps make fast work of deep cuts in tough materials. A variable-speed foot control allows you to keep your hands free to hold tools and work.

Hand-held motorized tool
Works much like a flex-shaft power carver, but more cumbersome because you hold motor housing in your hand. Less expensive than a flex-shaft carver.

High-speed steel cutter
Cut fast. Available in many shapes, and in tungsten-carbide for longer life.

Structured-tooth tungsten-carbide cutter
These bits make for controlled cutting because they work equally well with, and against, the grain.

Ruby cutter
Good for smoothing and carving intricate details.

Sanding drum
Many sizes and grits available for smoothing broad areas.

point (see the one in the carving tool guide on *page 10*).

• Two structured tooth bits: one that's long and thin such as the one shown in the carving tool guide on *page 10,* and another that's shorter, wider, and shaped like a barrel.

• Various sanding drums in coarse and fine grits.

Fred Cogelow: He brings large figure carvings to life

When you see a Fred Cogelow carving, it's hard not to be moved. Many of his carvings, such as the life size sculpture entitled "With Thoughts of Mabel," (see detail photo on *page 12)* convey a strong message about the lives of the rural people Fred has come to know

around his home in Willmar, Minnesota.

Fred keeps some 400 chisels and gouges in his shop, and another 50 or so knives, palm chisels, and dental picks within easy reach, so we weren't surprised when he hesitated before recommending a few essential tools.

continued

HOW TO SHOP SMART FOR CARVING TOOLS
continued

Fred Cogelow

preference for bent (spoon-shaped) blades. For example, the 7-piece Henry Taylor set contains one bent skew chisel, four bent gouges, and two back-bent gouges.

In place of a bench knife, Fred makes great use of a tool he calls the "Cogelow ½" bent skew," shown *below left,* for incision cuts. "By grasping the tool in one hand, and guiding the blade with two fingers of my other hand, I get all the control I need." You can purchase the tool from The Woodcraft Shop through the phone number in the box at *right.*

Sources for carving tools and literature:

•**Garrett Wade,** 212-807-1155
•**Ivan Whillock Studio,** 507-334-8306
•**Laughlin Woodcarving Supply,** 501-741-4757
•**The Woodcraft Shop,** 800-397-2278; 319-359-9684
•**Warren Tool Co.,** 914-876-7817
•**Wood Carvers Supply,** 804-583-8928
•**Woodcraft Supply,** 800-535-4482; 304-428-4866

"I'm a big believer in spoon gouges," Fred told us. "The spoon-shaped tools work well with a mallet, yet provide great accessibility to recessed areas. For the beginner, I recommend these spoon gouges: two No. 5s in ¼" and ¾" widths, a ½"-wide No. 9, and a ⅛"-wide No. 11. Also, a ¼" spoon-shaped V-parting tool will come in handy."

Because of the large size of most of his workpieces, Fred prefers tools with elongated handles. As he told us: "The palm handles just get in my way." And, he believes in buying well-made tools.

"It pays to buy high-quality brands, such as Ashley Iles, Henry Taylor, Hirsch/Two Cherries, or Swiss-made, because these tools will last a lifetime."

In fact, Henry Taylor manufactures several carving sets with tools forged to Fred's specifications. The tools in these sets reflect his

Fred Cogelow's life-size figure carvings have distinct personalities.

HOW TO SHARPEN TURNING AND CARVING TOOLS

Carving or turning wood with dull tools is like trying to cut tough steak with a butter knife. You simply don't get the desired results. To help you start sharp and stay sharp, we paid a visit to two accomplished craftsmen—one a turner, the other a carver—who know full well the value of sharp tools. Starting with turning tools, here's what they had to say about getting a good edge.

Tips for getting an edge on your turning tools

From this secluded shop in the northern woodlands of Wisconsin, Rus Hurt quietly turns objects of exquisite beauty. Many of these pieces will find their way into art galleries and juried shows. Not bad for someone who describes himself as "just another guy out in the tules who happens to turn well."

Rus especially enjoys passing along the secrets of his craft to aspiring turners at seminars and in one-on-one sessions in his own workshop. His first lesson: How to properly sharpen your turning

tools. Says Rus: "With dull tools you don't cut the wood; you tear it off, and that's how not to have fun with turning."

Determine the correct bevel and profile for your tools

After buying a turning tool, Rus regrinds its tip to match its intended purpose. "New tools are ground by machines that don't produce the necessary angles for smooth cutting," Rus said. "With most tools, the tips are too blunt,

so you have to lengthen the bevel and taper the profile slightly."

For example, the photos *below* show the degree to which Rus grinds away the ears of his gouges and increases the length of the bevels to match the work at hand. As you can see, he recommends using a long bevel when you're turning spindles, and a shorter one for bowl turning. If you use a single gouge for both purposes, a compromise such as the "general use" example will work well.

continued

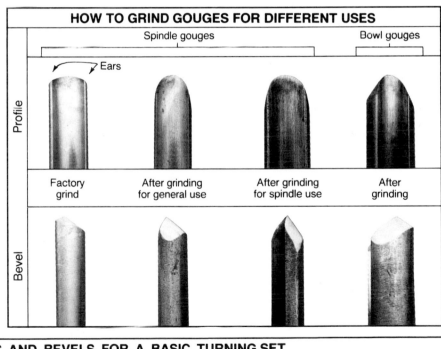

HOW TO GRIND GOUGES FOR DIFFERENT USES

Spindle gouges — Bowl gouges

Profile / Ears

| Factory grind | After grinding for general use | After grinding for spindle use | After grinding |

Bevel

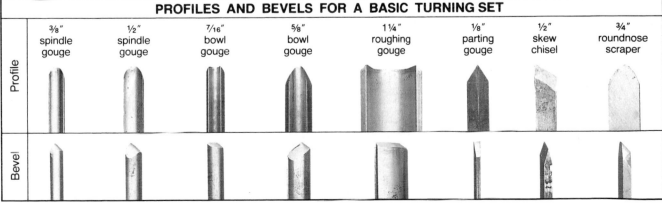

PROFILES AND BEVELS FOR A BASIC TURNING SET

	³⁄₈″ spindle gouge	½″ spindle gouge	⁷⁄₁₆″ bowl gouge	⁵⁄₈″ bowl gouge	1¼″ roughing gouge	⅛″ parting gouge	½″ skew chisel	¾″ roundnose scraper
Profile								
Bevel								

HOW TO SHARPEN TURNING AND CARVING TOOLS
continued

To show you how to grind a variety of turning tools, we asked this longtime turner to select eight basic tools (see photos on *page 13, bottom*). "With these tools, most turners can tackle 90 percent of all projects," he said.

Note: *Rus's bevel grinds should work well for you if you adjust the height of your lathe so the headstock center is about 1" above your elbow.*

Rough-grind your tool tips into shape

Using the photos on *page 13* as your guide, mark the necessary profile as shown at *right, top*. Then, hold the tip of the tool as shown at *right, bottom*, and grip its handle with your other hand.

After grinding the ears (outer corners of the edge) down to the line, grind the entire bevel in one smooth and continuous motion by swinging the handle in an arc and simultaneously rolling the tool's edge. The new profile should be a smooth arc, with equal amounts of steel removed from both sides. Try to minimize the number of facets (flat spots) on the bevel.

Put the final edge on the tool

With the tip now reshaped, you shouldn't have to rough-grind the tool again unless you nick or damage it in some way. You need only refine the bevel with the fine stone of your grinding wheel. Start by touching the heel of the bevel to the stone as shown *opposite, top left,* and ease the rest of the bevel into the grinding wheel. Smooth the entire bevel in a continuous arcing motion, and use a light touch. Again, aim for one continuous facet.

"I'm usually done at this point unless I'm turning a fragile burl or expensive piece of stock," said Rus. "In these instances, I'll hone the edge for an extra margin of sharpness." To do this, Rus gives the

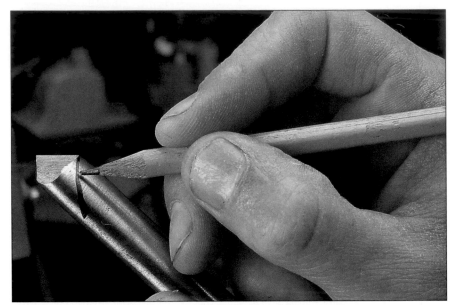
Before grinding, mark the tool's new profile with a pencil.

Keep the tool moving as you grind it to avoid overheating.

How to keep your tools cool when rough-grinding

Whenever you grind a tool, try not to overheat it. (When the steel turns blue, it has lost its temper and will not hold an edge.) Follow these pointers:

• Use a coarse stone.

• Keep the tool moving when it's against the stone.

• Be aggressive. Apply plenty of pressure to remove as much material as possible, then quickly get the tool off the stone before it overheats.

• Dip the tool in water frequently to lower its temperature.

• Because there's little steel near the cutting edge to dissipate heat, use a lighter touch when grinding near the tip.

• Practice your grinding on a piece of scrap steel. "I put in many hours at the grinding wheel before I became good," Rus reminded us, "and I still burn the steel occasionally."

Touch the heel of the bevel to the grinder first, then ease the toe into the wheel before grinding the entire bevel. This helps you avoid burning the edge.

With a slipstone you can quickly remove the burr from the edge of a gouge.

inside of the edge a few strokes with a coarse India slipstone as shown *above, far right* to remove the fine burr left from grinding. Then, he also strokes the bevel a few times as shown at *right*, rolling the tool as he pulls it.

Two more tips from Rus

"Buy high-speed steel (HSS) tools. You'll more than make up the higher cost in time saved from not having to resharpen them as much. And, HSS tools resist burning better than carbon-steel tools."

"Get in the habit of touching the tip of your turning tool with your finger each time you're ready to turn with it. The edge of a sharp tool will drag when you lightly run your thumb perpendicularly over the edge. You'll get a good feel for what 'sharp' means, and

continued

Stroke the tool's bevel several times with the flat side of a slipstone.

HOW TO SHARPEN TURNING AND CARVING TOOLS
continued

it could save you from damaging a turning with a dull tool. Just be careful not to cut yourself in the process!"

A proven system for sharpening carving tools

Harold Enlow, noted author and caricature carver, makes no bones about the importance of using sharp carving tools. "Some people complain that I put too much sharpening information in my books (he's published eight titles so far), but I ignore 'em because their tools are usually real dull," he told us with a chuckle.

Harold Enlow

To see firsthand Harold's tried-and-true sharpening technique, we paid a visit to his shop in the Ozark Mountains of northern Arkansas. Here's what we learned.

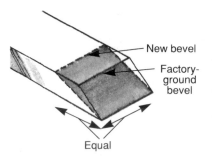

New bevel
Factory-ground bevel
Equal

If you carve softer woods, grind the bevel longer

"I would guess that 90 percent of the wood being carved is soft—mostly basswood," said Harold. "But most carving tools come with a short bevel that works OK with harder woods, but not with softer woods. After I grind the bevel longer, the tool slices through these soft woods much more easily, with no damage to the cutting edge."

Note: The following procedures work well with chisels, gouges, and bench knives. V-tools require special treatment (see page 17).

As shown in the drawing *below left,* Harold lengthens the bevel on chisels and gouges so it's equal to the width of the tool. To do this, use a coarse grinding wheel to remove steel from the bevel's heel. As you grind closer to the toe, be careful not to scorch the thin edge. (See the tips on *page 15* for more advice on keeping your tools cool.)

Your thumb helps steady the tool as you grind it, and also warns you when the tool gets too hot.

Harold guides the tool by grasping its handle in one hand, and putting downward pressure on the tool with the thumb of his other hand as shown *below, left.* This way, your thumb tells you when the tool gets too hot. When you're done grinding, there should be a slight burr on the edge (opposite the bevel surface). "At every stage of sharpening, I always feel for that fine burr. Then, and only then, can you be sure that you've reached the edge," Harold told us.

Hold the bevel flat on the stone as you stroke it heelfirst.

Use sharpening stones to flatten and smooth the bevel

Harold goes directly from the coarse grinding wheel to a coarse India bench stone to flatten the bevel and remove scratches. First, he applies an oil (motor oil or automatic-transmission fluid) to the stone and lays the bevel flat on the stone as shown *above.* "It's important that you apply plenty of pressure as you stroke the bevel several times," Harold said. "Your knuckles should turn white."

When working on a stone, remember to push and pull the tool for speedy metal removal. With gouges, you need to roll the tool as you push and pull it.

A note about the stones: "I use an India stone with a coarse and fine side, and a hard Arkansas stone, but most any combination of coarse, fine, and hard stones will work," Harold told us. "Other carvers get good results with diamond stones, water stones, you name it."

As you work, frequently check the tool's bevel in a strong sidelight. When most of the scratches disappear, switch to a fine stone. Harold repeats this process on the fine side of his India stone. When he's satisfied that he's removed all of the visible scratches, he removes the burr by stroking it lightly once or twice along the fine side of the stone. For gouges, use the long edge of the stone.

Next, Harold repeats everything he did on the fine side of the India stone on a hard Arkansas stone. "Some people skip this step and go directly to a strop [a leather strap with polishing compound on it] for the final honing, but this step saves you time on the strop. And, the less time you spend on the strop the better, because stropping tends to round the edge slightly."

The final step—stropping

To polish the edge and remove any traces of a burr, Harold strokes both sides of the cutting edge on a strop charged with Zam polishing compound (see the Buying Guide on *page 18* for a source). "You need to press hard and stroke each side of the tool five or six times," according to this seasoned carver. Because of its soft surface, you'll cut the strop if you try to push the tool across the leather, so only pull it along the surface.

As shown in the photo *top right,* Harold cuts off chunks of the compound and works it into his strop with the tool. When the Zam turns black, you'll need to add more compound. Polish the concave edge of a gouge by rolling it along the edge of the strop as shown *right.*

How to tell when to resharpen your carving tools

To check his tools for sharpness, Harold shaves a few hairs off his arm. If the hairs don't shave easily, he gives the tool a few more

strokes on the strop. Just be careful not to cut yourself.

Harold finds that he can restrop a tool two or three times before taking it back to the fine-India-stone stage of his sharpening process. "You don't have to go back to the grinder or coarse India stone unless the tool gets accidentally nicked."

How to get your V-tools shipshape

"In my seminars I find that few people know how to sharpen a V-tool," Harold said. "You can get by with a chisel or knife that's half-dull, but a V-tool has to be perfect or it'll give you fits."

To achieve victory with your V-tool, follow the sharpening
continued

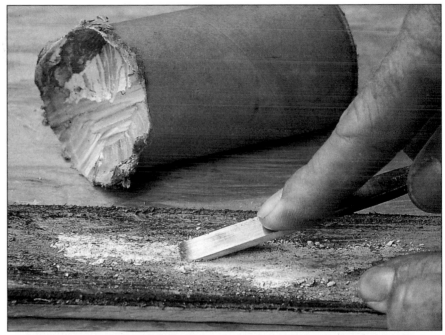

As you strop the tool, mash the bits of compound into the leather surface. Press hard as you pull the tool along the strop five or six times.

Roll the concave side of a gouge as you pull it along the strop's edge. For each stroke, roll the tool completely from one corner of the edge to the other.

HOW TO SHARPEN TURNING AND CARVING TOOLS
continued

sequence for other carving tools, but with these differences:

• First, you need to check the V-tool's edge for squareness. If it looks like the example shown on the left side of the illustration *below,* you'll need to grind it square as shown on the right side of the same drawing. As also shown in this drawing, you should lengthen the bevels so they equal the width of one side of the V.

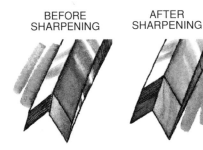

BEFORE SHARPENING   AFTER SHARPENING

• Check to make sure that the two edges of the tool meet in a perfect V as shown in the "After sharpening" example *below.* (You may need a magnifying glass and strong light.) If they don't, you'll need to grind them into shape.

BEFORE SHARPENING	AFTER SHARPENING
Bevels don't line up	Grind bevels so they are even
Bevel length is short	Equal / Increase bevel length

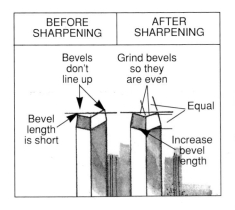

• Doing this may prove impossible if the channel machined down the shank of the tool isn't centered as shown *above right.* So, check your V-tools for this defect before purchasing them.

Channel not centered

• On small V-tools, you may want to skip the grinding-wheel stage and only work on India stones to help you maintain control over steel removal.

• Use thin, hard Arkansas slipstones to remove the burr on V-tools as shown *below.* For small V-tools, Harold sharpens and shapes his slipstone on an India stone to make the slipstone's edge fit into the V.

The inside of the V should have some roundness, so slightly round over the outside of the V on a fine India stone to match the inside as shown *right top.*

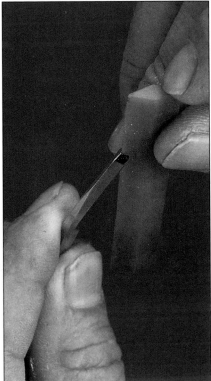

A slipstone with a fine point helps you deburr the inside edge of a V-tool.

Gently round the outside of the V on a fine India stone, so it matches the roundness on the inside of the V.

To polish the inside surface of a V-tool, pull it along the strop's edge.

To polish the inside surfaces of the V-tool, stroke it along the edge of a strop as shown *above.*

Buying guide
• **Zam polishing compound.** For current price, contact Laughlin Woodcarving Supply, Route 6, Box 147, Harrison, AR 72601, or call 501-741-4757.
• **Two-sided India stone.** One 8x2x1" coarse/fine stone. Item No. 08M04.01. For current price, contact Garrett Wade, 161 Avenue of the Americas, New York, NY 10013, or call 800-221-2942. (All types of sharpening accessories available. Call 212-807-1155 for information.)

PUT A SUPER-FINE EDGE ON YOUR CARVING TOOLS

Nothing raises the frustration level of a beginning carver more than using dull tools, which make carving dangerous as well as difficult. Carving, however, can be safe and enjoyable if you know how to use the one tool that carvers always keep at arm's length—the leather strop.

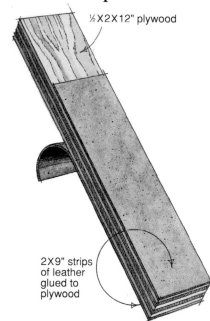

½X2X12" plywood

2X9" strips of leather glued to plywood

1. You can buy a variety of strops, in prices from $15 to $40, but after talking with some prominent carvers, we're convinced that all you need is an easy-to-make, two-sided leather strop and two different pastes. You can buy coarse (emery), and medium (tripoli) pastes from the source in the Buying Guide at the end of this article.

To make a strop like the one shown *above,* cut a 2X12" piece of ½" plywood, then glue 2X9" strips of belt leather (available from the Buying Guide source) to both sides of the plywood. Attach the leather strips to the same end of the plywood stick to leave a 3" handle at the other end.

2. Now, apply coarse paste to one of the leather strips, and medium paste to the other strip. To sharpen a bench knife, hold the strop (coarse side up) in one hand, and the knife, with its sharp edge facing away from you, in your other hand. Set the blade onto the far end of the strop, with the back edge of the tool just off the leather surface as shown *above.* Press down on the knife and pull it toward you. Now, stroke the opposite side of the blade back down the strop and repeat this step 10–12 times. Then, repeat this process on the medium compound.

3. To sharpen a gouge, hold one end of the tool's edge against the coarse surface of the strop as shown *above.* As you pull the gouge toward you, roll it so all of the cutting edge makes contact with the strop during one stroke. Repeat this stroke 10–12 times. Always pull the gouge toward you—pushing the sharp edge into the leather will cut the strop. Then, flip over the strop and repeat this process on its medium side.

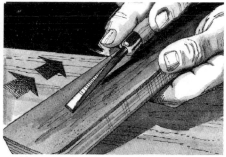

4. Sharpen a V-tool by first stroking one side of the V, then the other on the coarse compound. Next, lay the point of the V on the strop as shown *above,* and pull the tool toward you 5–6 times. Repeat this process on the medium compound.

5. Stropping will form a microscopic burr on the unbeveled (or inside) edge of both the gouge and V-tool. Remove the burr by placing the unbeveled edge of the tool along the corner of the strop as shown *above.* Then, pull the tool toward you 3 times and repeat this process on the other side of the strop.

Buying Guide
• **Belt leather.** 2x36" strip, item No. 4534. For current price, contact Tandy Leather Co., PO Box 2934, Dept. WO289, Fort Worth, TX 76101.

•**Emery compound.** Item No. 07M03. Item No. 01T41. For current price, contact Woodcraft, 210 Wood County Industrial Park, P.O. Box 1686, Parkersburg, WV 26102, or call 800-225-1153.

HOLLOW-GRIND SHARPENING

We put a lot of miles on our cutting tools here in the *WOOD*® workshop, so we do more than an average amount of tool sharpening. You would never catch any of us saying that restoring a beat-up cutting edge to its original keen state is our idea of a good time. Still, we all agree that there's no good reason why any woodworker can't sharpen many shop tools.

You don't sharpen all tools using the same techniques because each tool category requires different strategies. (See the previous two articles for tips on sharpening other tools, and incidentally, we never sharpen carbide-tipped cutters.) But you can renew several types of shop tools—chisels, plane irons, jointer knives, and lathe chisels— by first *hollow-grinding* the cutting edge then *honing,* or refining, the edge further with a honing guide and a stone of some sort.

We honestly don't think that sharpening the tools mentioned represents too great a challenge. But as you might expect, it helps to be aware of a few tricks of the sharpening trade. That's what this article is all about.

What you'll need to do the job

When we gathered all the items we use to hollow-grind our tools, we were surprised by how little equipment we need. Of course, you'll need a *bench grinder* or one of the slow-speed grinders now available on the market. (We use the former.) Also mandatory is a *dressing stick* or a *dressing wheel* to true up the *grinding wheel.* If you try to hollow-grind a cutting edge with a wheel that hasn't been "dressed," the results won't please you. Speaking of wheels, we use a 60-grit (medium-fine) aluminum oxide wheel because it runs fairly cool and doesn't clog with metal shavings too rapidly.

You'll also want to round up a *try square,* an *awl,* and a felt-tip *marker* or some *machinists' ink* to mark the cutting edge for grinding.

And to ensure accuracy during the honing process, we depend on a *honing guide* to control the angle of the cutting edge against the sharpening stone. While you hear of some people who say they can steady a plane iron well enough to maintain the original bevel angle, we prefer the honing guide. You can buy this tool almost anywhere for around $10 or less.

We also use two *waterstones*— a 1,000-grit and a 6,000-grit—to hone the cutting edges of our tools. Some people insist on oilstones for honing, but we like the speed and the results we get with waterstones.

If you're sharpening any woodturning gouges, you'll need a *slipstone* similar to the one shown later in this article. This tool removes the burr that grinding produces on the inside surface of the gouge.

Since hollow-grind sharpening involves the use of a bench grinder in most instances, we always wear eye and face protection to prevent accidents involving sparks or flying slivers of tool steel. And to keep the steel cool during grinding, you need a quench tray nearby. A small dish full of water will suffice.

A few words about our sharpening jig

We discovered something important while researching this article. To grind tools successfully, you must have a support system for controlling the removal of steel from the cutting edge. True, all bench grinders have a tool rest designed for this purpose. Frankly, though, we haven't found them sturdy enough or large enough to do the job well in all cases. That's why we developed the jig shown *below.*

continued

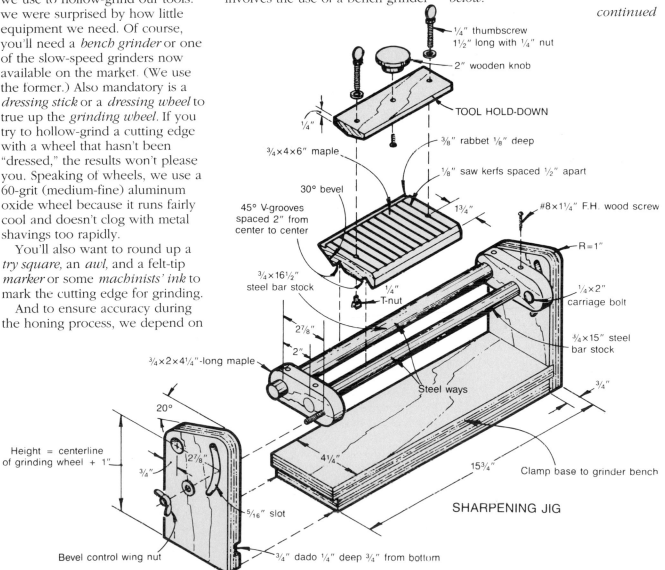

¼" thumbscrew 1½" long with ¼" nut

2" wooden knob

TOOL HOLD-DOWN

¾×4×6" maple

¼"

30° bevel

45° V-grooves spaced 2" from center to center

⅜" rabbet ⅛" deep

⅛" saw kerfs spaced ½" apart

1¾"

#8×1¼" F.H. wood screw

R=1"

¾×16½" steel bar stock

¼" T-nut

¼×2" carriage bolt

¾×15" steel bar stock

2⅞"

2"

¾×2×4¼"-long maple

Steel ways

¾"

20°

Height = centerline of grinding wheel + 1"

2⅞"

¾"

4¼"

15¾"

Clamp base to grinder bench

Bevel control wing nut

⁵⁄₁₆" slot

¾" dado ¼" deep ¾" from bottom

SHARPENING JIG

21

HOLLOW-GRIND SHARPENING
continued

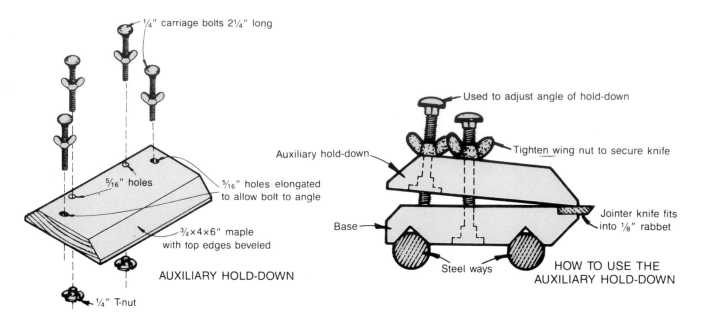

¼" carriage bolts 2¼" long

⁵⁄₁₆" holes

⁵⁄₁₆" holes elongated
to allow bolt to angle

¾×4×6" maple
with top edges beveled

AUXILIARY HOLD-DOWN

¼" T-nut

Used to adjust angle of hold-down

Auxiliary hold-down

Tighten wing nut to secure knife

Base

Jointer knife fits
into ⅛" rabbet

Steel ways

**HOW TO USE THE
AUXILIARY HOLD-DOWN**

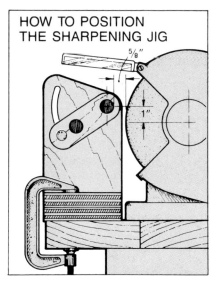

**HOW TO POSITION
THE SHARPENING JIG**

⅝"

1"

We think the sketches presented do a pretty good job of showing how to construct the jig, so we won't belabor the point. However, there are a few things you should know about this contraption.

First off, we made the jig wide enough to provide adequate support along the entire length of the cutting edge being ground. And to prevent movement, which could cause the edge to be ground unevenly, we used ¾" steel rod for the ways of the jig. For the same reason, we made it possible for you

to lock the adjustable bevel guide easily at both ends.

Note also the kerfs in the tool hold-down base. These make it easier for you to set the cutting edge of the tool perpendicular to the grinding wheel.

We made two interchangeable hold-downs for the base that slides along the ways of the jig. Which of these you fasten to the base depends on the tool being ground. For all tools except jointer knives, use the one shown immediately above the base in the sketch at right. With jointer knives, you'll need the auxiliary hold-down. The two sketches *above* show how to construct the auxiliary hold-down and how to clamp it to the base.

You can clamp the jig to a workbench in front of your grinder, if you wish, or to a wooden base that's been fastened between the grinder and the metal stand.

Hollow grinding: The essential first step

Actually, there are only two ways to sharpen tools of any kind. You can either hollow-grind and hone them, or you can flat-grind them (that's what the pros do with router

bits, for example). In the case of the tools under discussion here—chisels, plane irons, jointer knives, and lathe tools—hollow grinding is the best way to go. Why? Because hollow grinding speeds the sharpening process by removing the center portion of steel between the toe (front) and heel (back) of the bevel. This translates into less time spent honing later on. The concave surface also allows a certain amount of clearance for removal of wood shavings.

The following sequence shows you how we go about grinding a square edge on a cutting tool. As we progress through the procedure, we think you'll see how important a role the jig plays.

1. Sometimes, no matter how careful you are with cutting tools, they get rusty or otherwise "gunked up." To clean and shine metal surfaces, we use a flap sander. It's fast and effective, and it makes the steel look almost like new. Tool steel is pretty hard stuff, so you don't have to worry about the flap sander ruining the tool. You needn't sand the beveled cutting edge this way, though. You'll take care of it during grinding.

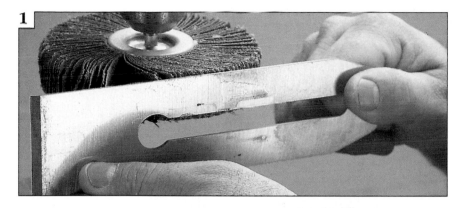

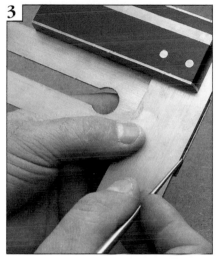

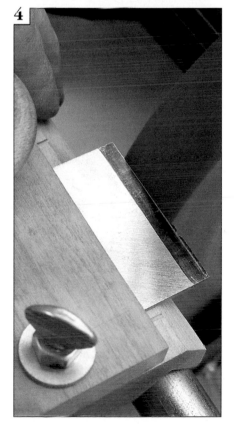

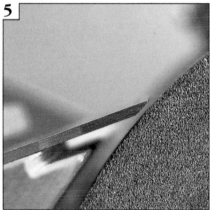

this type of product at most machinery supply outlets.)

3. As a cutting tool does its work, it inevitably picks up its share of nicks and cuts along the way. To remove them, first we "paint" the end of the tool with a felt-tip pen. (The pros prefer machinists' ink. One bottle of this ink will last a lifetime.) Then, we use a try square and an awl to scribe the line to which we want to grind. Remember that you want the scribe line behind all the nicks.

4. Next, capture the cutter in the tool hold-down, lower the hold-down onto the steel ways, and adjust the bevel guide so the wheel will grind off the unwanted metal at about a 90° angle to the cutting edge. Carefully position the cutter so that the wheel will only remove the desired amount of metal. Then, exert a little downward pressure on the hold-down, and move the cutter back and forth across the wheel. Don't hurry! (The sketch *opposite* shows how to construct the auxiliary hold-down and how to secure jointer knives for grinding.)

5. Once you've squared up the edge, loosen the tool hold-down thumbscrews and the wing nuts that control the bevel guide angle and adjust the bevel guide to the correct grinding angle. Take a look at your setup from the side to make sure that the angle of grind is correct. Keep in mind that you want to retain the original bevel angle of the cutter. Remember also that the bevel angle on every tool has been designed (and set at the factory) for maximum cutting efficiency. Changing the angle appreciably will result in a less-than-desired cutting action.

6. When you're sure the bevel is set correctly, slide the tool's cutting edge forward until it makes contact with the grinding wheel. Tighten the holddown thumbscrews, turn on the grinder, and move the tool across the wheel. You may have to slide the cutting edge forward again to remove the desired amount of steel. (The object is to completely remove the squared-off edge.) Dip
continued

2. Earlier, we mentioned the importance of your grinding wheel being squared up. To effect that, we secure our dressing stick in the hold down as shown and move it back and forth across the wheel a few times. The dressing stick also removes the "glaze," which actually is a buildup of metal embedded in the wheel's surface. (We use a Norton 37C24-TVK dressing stick. You can purchase

HOLLOW-GRIND SHARPENING
continued

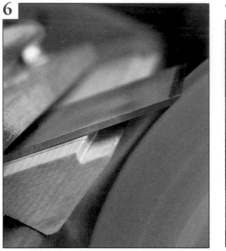

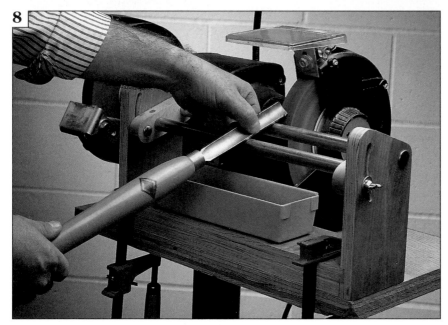

the tool in your quench tray frequently to keep the metal from losing temper. If you don't, the cutter will lose its edge quickly during use.

7. One good way to tell that the edge is ready for honing is to hold the tool as shown here and lightly pass it over your fingernail. If it grabs easily and shaves the nail, you're there.

8. When hollow-grinding turning gouges, we use a different procedure. We position the bevel guide at the angle that matches that of the

gouge, move the gouge forward until the metal meets the wheel, and roll the gouge from the center toward each side. Notice that we steady the gouge with one hand and roll the tool with the other. This procedure takes a certain amount of getting used to. Here again, remove only a little steel at a time, and be sure to quench the steel at frequent intervals.

9. The grinding process creates a burr along the inside of the cutting edge. You will want to remove this to ensure the sharpest possible

cutting edge. A couple of passes with a slipstone, as shown, will remove the unwanted burr.

Honing: How to put a razor-sharp edge on your hollow-ground tools

It would be great if all you had to do to renew a tired cutting edge was hollow-grind it. Unfortunately, there's more to the story than that. Honing picks up where hollow-grinding leaves off. It transforms a "pretty sharp" edge into a "razor-sharp woodshearing machine."

hold the blade with the flat side down and make a few circular passes over the stone as shown in the sketch. Since you will need to hone both the beveled cutting edge and the flat back side of the blade several times, make sure you keep the honing guide secured to the blade during the entire process. Otherwise, you'll spend lots of time trying to adjust the honing guide angle.

Note: When we're sharpening jointer knives or lathe chisels. we don't feel that it is necessary to hone the cutting edge with a stone finer than the 1,000-grit waterstone. Why? Because both of these types of tools do their cutting with the help of a power tool, which means that the edge needn't be as sharp as if the tool is hand-powered. But with wood chisels and plane irons, we repeat Steps 1, 2, and 3 with a 6,000-grit waterstone. Going the extra distance will pay big dividends, especially when you call on your tool to cut through hardwoods.

Actually, honing is a several-step process in which you alternately sharpen the front and back surfaces of the cutting edge. The photos, drawings, and captions that follow show how we hone hollow-ground tools.

1. As mentioned earlier, we use waterstones to hone our tools. Because waterstones wear away quickly when used, you need to make sure that the surface of the stone is flat before you use it. We lay a sheet of wet/dry abrasive on a piece of plate glass, sprinkle water on the abrasive, and then slide our premoistened stone over the abrasive several times. We use plate glass because of its reputation for being flat.

correctly, you need to make sure that you position the tool being sharpened in it so that both the toe and heel of the cutting edge rest on the stone (see the drawing *above* for how it should look). Move the cutting edge back and forth along the stone several times. (If you're honing a jointer knife or a lathe chisel, you'll have to maintain the angle free-hand.)

3. Every time you hone one surface of the cutting edge, you create a burr on the opposite surface. To remove the burr,

2. To make sure the stone doesn't move around, we capture it in a simple jig. When honing wood chisels and plane irons, we enlist the help of a honing guide. For one of these tools to perform

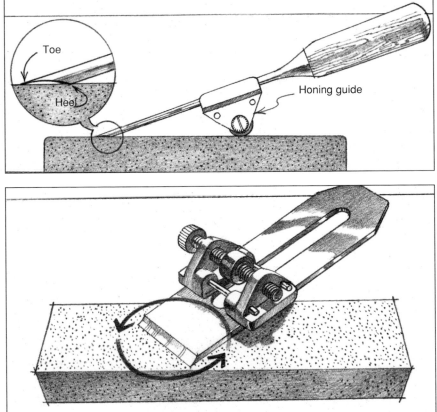

ROUGHOUTS TO THE RESCUE

Let's face it—not everyone can visualize a figure and sculpt it from a block of wood. That's why many woodcarvers now start with a roughout, a partially completed, machine carved figure with the rough shaping and proportioning already done. Here's a look at machine-made roughout: where they started, how they're made, and what they can—or cannot— do for you.

Helping the pros produce

For years, professional carvers selling to the wholesale and retail trade have relied on machine-made roughouts. They're the secret behind selling carvings profitably, according to Ron Conn of Ozark Mountain Crafts in Branson, Missouri. His firm manufactures roughouts for pros and amateurs alike and markets a line of finished carvings to retailers.

"Carvers doing work for stores are aiming at a price range; they have to work as economically as

Cigar store Indian and raccoon, Ozark Mountain Crafts; coyote, Rossiter Ruff-outs and Carving Supplies. For information, see the Buying Guide on *page 29.*

they can," Ron explains. So, while machines grind away at the grunt work, the carver concentrates on the final form and details. "Each piece takes less time, but still has the individuality people expect in a hand-carving," Ron says.

Machined roughouts turn up in classes as teaching aids, too. By zeroing in on finishing and detailing techniques, some instructors say, students sharpen their skills in less class time. And students have the satisfaction of taking home a completed carving when the course is over.

Roughouts at retail

The popularity of roughouts has carved out several businesses in the last few years. Ivan and Trudy Rossiter, for instance, started manufacturing and marketing roughouts about four years ago. Since then, Rossiter Ruff-outs and Carving Supply (formerly Duplication by the Dozen) in Wichita, Kansas, has grown right along with the carving population.

"We started with about 50 models; now we have 200 or so," Ivan says. "We're always looking for new designs. We need to add 50 or 60 new ones to our catalog every year to keep up with demand." Some carvers allow the Rossiters to sell roughouts of their designs in exchange for a quantity of them. In addition, a customer can have any number of roughouts made from a carving—to make a series for sale or gifts, for instance. Keeping up with the carvers can consume 3,000 to 5,000 board feet of northern basswood each month. So, people in the roughout business are

Harold Davis carves a dozen goose heads at Ozark Mountain Crafts.

sensitive to changes in the market. "Basswood prices are high now," roughout-maker Conn says. "Rough logs are selling overseas for what we used to pay for milled lumber," he adds. He deals with several suppliers, buying truckloads of RWL lumber (random widths and lengths) of a specified grade and moisture content (6 percent).

Old techniques for modern times

The machines and techniques that now hew out carving roughouts came from the furniture industry, commercial woodworking, and even shoemaking. The technology isn't new. Mechanized production carving of items as diverse as shoe lasts (the foot-shaped forms shoemakers use), fireplace mantels, table legs, waterfowl decoys, and foundry patterns has been going on for a century or more.

"Carousel horses are a direct link to carving's industrial past," Ron says. Once, they were carved completely by hand. But by the

Sidney Clevenger laminates stock for some roughouts. This hydraulic press will clamp pieces up to 24X24X60".

1920s, commercial pressures had forced most makers to turn to a hybrid process that parallels the way today's carvers use roughouts—hand finishing of machine-made rough carvings.

"These machines came out of a furniture factory, and we rebuilt them," he says, pointing to two duplicating carvers in his building. One machine makes four copies at a time of work up to 7' long—it once made fireplace mantels. The other one, shown *above, top* makes a

dozen copies at a time of smaller patterns.

On either machine, the roughouts start from a master pattern, the three-dimensional wood or metal original to be duplicated. "We can make a wooden master right on the machine from a finished carving, a rough carving, or even a clay model," Ron explains. "We have metal masters made for our high-

continued

ROUGHOUTS TO THE RESCUE
continued

volume carvings because they last longer."

The master mounts on the duplicator much like a turning mounts between centers on a lathe. The blocks of wood destined to become roughouts also mount between centers, parallel to the master and arrayed alongside it, as shown in the machine photo. A bar—suspended so it can move to either side, front to back, and up or down—spans the master and the blocks. Then, the machine operator manipulates the bar so that a stylus on it traces the surface of the master.

Above each block location, a spindle on the bar holds a rotating

Baseball player, Otto the otter, and bear roughouts from Rossiter Ruff-outs and Carving Supply, address *opposite*.

bit, similar to a router bit. It cuts away the block surface to match the profile traced by the stylus. Mechanical linkage between the mounting centers holding the master and the blocks enables the operator to rotate them to different positions simultaneously to cut from different angles, thus covering the entire surface.

After one pass, the operator can change to a smaller bit to carve finer detail, if necessary. The level of detail put into a blank depends on who's going to be using the completed roughout—an amateur or a professional.

"Professional carvers don't like a blank that's cut too close; they want to have enough room to give each carving some personality," Ron comments. "Roughouts for general sale are usually cut closer to the finished carving."

A pair of hydraulically operated high-speed duplicating lathes in the

shop came from the shoemaking industry, where they carved shoe lasts. Ron has carved shoetrees, decoy bodies, and rolling pins, among other things, on the Italian-made machines.

A legacy of their shoemaking origins, they can create proportionally enlarged or reduced copies of three-dimensional patterns. So, a small carving pattern can be made quickly into something much bigger—just like the roughout business itself.

Roughouts have drawbacks, too

When carousel-horse manufacturers blended machine carving with hand finishing 70 years ago to speed up production and cut costs, they also opened the work to a wider range of people. Carousel-horse carvers no longer needed the ability to sculpt a horse. Working with machine-carved blanks, they needed only to detail and finish the horse.

Professional carvers today continue to enjoy the commercial advantages of roughouts. But, it's the ease roughouts bring to carving that's helping push them to new heights of popularity. For some hobbyists, it's the only way to carve.

Like assembling a model airplane kit, finishing and detailing a rough-out provides hours of pleasure and relaxation. By starting the job with important shapes and proportions already established, novice carvers can avoid the disappointment of carving a deer that looks more like a moose.

But some carvers warn that there's a danger in leaning too heavily on roughouts, especially for anyone who wants to pursue carving seriously. "Roughouts speed up a project, and they work fine for someone who wants to do only details," woodcarver and instructor Dave Rushlo of Scottsdale, Arizona, says.

Patterns line shelves at Ozark Mountain Crafts. The popular boot pattern on the middle shelf is made of metal to resist wear.

Gene Clevenger finishes a carved boot for retail sale. Carvers note: He's using a pounce pattern wheel to simulate stitching.

But he adds, "To become a good carver, you need to know how to lay out a carving. You should pick your subject and keep working at it. You should develop your own style." That's particularly important advice for anybody who plans to enter carving competitions, since many shows and contests bar carvings made from roughouts.

Roughout makers Ron Conn and Ivan Rossiter agree in part with the Arizona carver. But, they say, roughouts are just the thing for the 80 or 90 percent of carvers who are in it purely for enjoyment. "It's true, you're always working on someone else's design," Ron says, "but not everyone is able to, or even wants to, draw up an original design, plan the carving, saw the blank, rough it out, and finish it." Adds Ivan, "Many people just don't have much time for carving. Roughouts let them spend the time they do have on the most enjoyable part of the job."

Buying Guide

Here are some firms that supply carving roughouts. Call or write for a catalog.

•**Blanks of waterfowl, fish, and songbirds.** Big Sky Carvers, 8256 Huffine Lane, Bozeman, MT 59715, 406-586-0008.

•**Game birds, songbirds, birds of prey.** Custom roughouts. Dupli-Tech, Eric Farner, Box 51, Charleroi, PA 15022, 412-483-8883.

•**European-style precarved Nativity scene.** Huggler-Wyss America, Inc., 541 SW Pacific Ave., Willmar, MN 56201, 612-235-6020.

•**General line of figure, caricature, and wildlife blanks.** Laughlin's Wood Carving Supplies, Rt. 6, Box 147 Harrison, AR 72601, 501-741-4757.

•**General line of figure, caricature, and wildlife blanks.** Ozark Mountain Crafts, Box R Branson, MO 65616, 417-561-8275.

•**Figure, caricature, and wildlife blanks.** Custom roughouts. Rossiter Ruff-outs and Carving Supply, 1447 S. Santa Fe, Wichita, KS 67211, 800-8-BLANKS.

•**Figure and animal blanks with reference casts.** Wetherbee Studio, Rich Wetherbee, 3370 N. El Paso, Unit Q, Colorado Springs, CO 80907.

Hobo, cowboy, and cowgirl caricatures; Nativity figures. Wood Carvers Supply, Inc., Box 75006, Englewood, FL 34295-7500, 800-AT HOBBY.

THE WOODS THAT CARVERS CRAVE

Your tools and what you carve will determine the wood.

Basswood, butternut, catalpa, tupelo—experienced carvers recognize these woods as old friends. They know their attributes, quirks, and temperaments. Beginners who select the wrong wood for their projects, though, may never want to carve again. Here are some tips on choosing a carving wood and a guide to the popular species.

The well-honed woodcarver knows the importance of selecting the right wood. After all, a lot of time will be spent with that piece of wood before the carving emerges. And what a disappointment if it doesn't turn out quite right! That's why any carver will tell you that it pays to know your silent partner.

What to look for in wood

Sometimes, just for the heck of it, you want to carve a specific piece of wood for a project, regardless of the stock's qualities: a spoon carved from the pruned limb of a backyard apple tree, for instance. Perhaps you find a great piece of driftwood on vacation and decide to make something from it. Neither of these woods may be ideal for carving, but in these instances, it's the source that's special. Most times, though, you'll want to remember these guidelines:

• *Always select well-seasoned wood.* Green, moisture-laden wood likely will crack and check as it dries, leaving unwanted flaws in your work. So, carve either kiln- or air-dried stock, but mostly, leave green wood alone.

• *Carve only straight-grained and knot-free stock.* Unless you're an advanced carver striving for a special effect, avoid burls and other figure with twisted, unpredictable grain that leads edges astray.

• *Choose wood that suits your carving method.* A small, handheld, whittling project typically requires softer wood than a piece that you secure in a vise and carve with gouges and a mallet. If power-carving suits your interest, realize that your equipment, fitted with the right cutters, probably can tackle the toughest woods.

• *Keep the finish in mind.* Light colored, featureless wood demands paint or stain. Stock with breath-taking color and grain looks best with a natural finish that won't compete with the wood.

• *What you carve counts, too.* A cowboy caricature probably would look odd in oil-finished walnut, as would a modern, flowing sculpture decked out in multicolored paint.

Now that you know some of the reasoning that underlies the selection of wood for a carving, look at the chart, *opposite,* and see what each species has to offer you. Remember, all of them have a following among carvers.

12 TOP CARVING WOODS

	TYPE OF WOOD	GRAIN	HARDNESS	COMMENTS	USES	FINISH	AVAILABILITY	COST
	BASSWOOD (Tilia americana)	Tight Straight Uniform	Soft	Takes detail	Figures Relief Signs Wildlife	Paint Stain	Common	Inexpensive
	BUTTERNUT (Juglans cinerea)	Straight Semi-open	Medium	Takes detail Getting harder to find	Figures Relief Sculpture Signs Furniture	Natural Stain	Regional	Moderate
	CATALPA, NORTHERN (Catalpa speciosa)	Tight Twisted Figured	Medium	Noncommercial; obtain from local sources	Figures Sculpture	Natural Stain	Regional	Inexpensive
	CHERRY (Prunus serotina)	Tight Straight Uniform	Extreme hardness	Avoid sap pockets Takes fine detail	Relief Sculpture Furniture Architectural trim	Natural	Common	Moderate
	COTTONWOOD (Populus sp.)	Tight Straight Uniform	Soft	Fuzzes	Figures	Paint Stain	Regional	Inexpensive
	HONDURAS MAHOGANY (Swietenia mac.)	Tight Straight Uniform	Hard	Takes fine detail	Relief Sculpture Furniture Architectural trim	Natural	Common	Expensive
	JELUTONG (Dyera costulata)	Tight Straight Uniform	Soft	Sap pockets Takes fine detail	Figures Wildlife	Paint Stain	Common	Expensive
	OAK, RED (Quercus rubra)	Open Straight Uniform	Hard	Splinters Chips Needs filling	Relief Signs Furniture Architectural trim	Natural Stain	Common	Moderate
	PINE, SUGAR/WHITE (Pinus lambertiana, strobus)	Tight Straight Uniform	Soft	Takes fine detail	Figures Relief Signs Wildlife	Paint Stain	Common	Inexpensive
	REDWOOD (Sequoia sempervirens)	Tight Straight Uniform	Soft	Splinters Chips	Sculpture Signs	Natural	Common	Moderate
	TUPELO (Nyssa aquatica)	Tight Straight Uniform	Soft	Takes fine detail	Figures Wildlife	Paint Stain	Regional	Moderate
	WALNUT (Juglans nigra)	Semi-open Straight	Medium	Splinters	Relief Sculpture Signs Furniture Architectural trim	Natural	Common	Expensive

CARVING TIPS AND TECHNIQUES

Here are carving techniques that will help you take a project from rough-hewn to reality in a series of simple steps. With complete information on form as well as function, you'll be carving objects to treasure in no time.

STEP-BY-STEP RELIEF CARVING

If you've ever admired a beautiful relief carving, but thought you weren't artistic enough to try it, think again! Even those of us with little or no eye for proportion or sculpture can be successful . . . once we know a few of the rules. Here's your chance to get the basic instruction that will allow you to dive right in and come up a winner.

A carver by any other name

Jim Rose didn't know anything about carving when he and his wife, Pam, spotted some relief carvings at a theme park. When Pam wanted to buy a caricature of an Ozark Mountain man, Jim responded like so many of us by saying "I can do that." The scene happened 20 years ago, and Jim's been carving away ever since, winning awards and the respect of fellow carvers.

While many of us at *WOOD*® magazine dabble in carving, we turned to this resident of Ankeny, Iowa, for some expert advice. Jim was happy to help us, with one regret: "I wish this article had been written when I was starting out—I had to learn the hard way, by myself."

The "big 5" tools: All you need to start

Some relief carvers carry around suitcases full of carving tools, but you can make 90 percent of all the cuts you'll ever need with five basic tools. So, we suggest you postpone the purchase of more elaborate tools until the need arises. We also recommend that you buy pre-sharpened tools that only need an occasional stropping to stay sharp. To learn how to use a strop, see the short article on *page 19.*

Here's a list of the five tools shown *below,* and what each will do for you. Refer to the glossary for unfamiliar terms. See the Buying Guide on *page 37* if you'd like to purchase this set.

• *Bench knife.* We like the Stanley Slimknife because of its retractable blade that's thin yet sturdy. Use the knife for making stop cuts and for cleaning up loose shavings. You can use an X-acto knife in its place, but we had our best results with the Stanley model.

• *⅜" No. 12 V-tool.* A great little tool for making outlining cuts and textured lines such as hair or veins.

• *⅜" No. 5 Gouge.* This tool makes fast work of wasting a lot of stock, removing wood up to a stop cut, and for texturing shapes such as a wave background.

• *⅜" No. 1 Straight chisel.* You'll find yourself reaching for a straight chisel when you need to flatten or round over a surface, or to remove coarse tool marks.

• *⅜" No. 1 Skew chisel.* Primarily used for rounding over edges, you'll also use the fine point of a skew chisel to remove material from tight areas.

In carving, it helps to know the language

Relief carvers have a vocabulary all their own, so we couldn't resist including some of the most-often-used words in this article:

• *Bench hook.* This simple device secures a workpiece in place while you carve. We show you how to make one on *page 34.*

• *Outlining cut.* The first cut you'll make (see Step 2 on *page 35),* it forms a groove around the design, separating the raised portion of the pattern from the background.

• *Stop cut.* Usually made with a straight downward plunge of a knife, this cut forms a vertical gap that *stops* a second cut made at a horizontal angle. Step 6 on *page 36* shows a stop cut.

• *Strop.* A strip of leather treated with a buffing compound used for sharpening blades.

• *Under cut.* To help the three-dimensional quality of a relief carving, these cuts remove stock from underneath the outside edges
continued

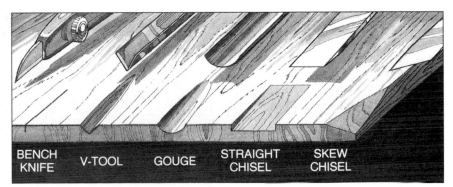

BENCH KNIFE   V-TOOL   GOUGE   STRAIGHT CHISEL   SKEW CHISEL

STEP-BY-STEP RELIEF CARVING
continued

of the design, just as we do in Steps 15 and 16 on *page 37*.

• *Wasting*. Refers to the removal of a large amount of stock, usually in taking out the background material around a design with a gouge (see step 10 on *page 36*).

Get a good grip

You'll carve safer and more effectively if you hold the tools correctly. For an ideal grip on chisels, gouges, and V-tools, hold them as shown on *pages 35–36*, with the butt end of the handle firmly planted in your palm. For maximum accuracy, guide the tool with the index and middle fingers of your free hand. Hold your knife much like you would a pencil, as shown *below*.

Placing your index finger on the top of knife allows you to put downward pressure on the blade.

"I can tell if someone's a beginning carver because their fingertips and knuckles turn white when they hold the tool," Jim Rose told us. "They should be pushing the tool with their arm and shoulder, not their fingers."

The carving motion: Like scooping ice cream

For safe, controlled, and accurate cuts, use the basic motion shown *above right* to remove wood. Push the tool into the project at a 25–30° angle, then lower your wrist as you

make the cut, with the tool nearly parallel to the wood surface as the blade lifts out of the wood. For fast wasting around the outside of a pattern, as shown in Step 10 on *page 36*, start the tool at a 45–50° angle.

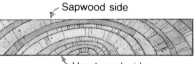

Keep your blades sharp

Nothing will frustrate you more quickly than dull tools. That's why experienced carvers constantly resharpen their tools for quality cuts. Because it takes more force to push a dull tool through wood than a sharp one, dull edges can also lead to injury. Why? By exerting unnecessary force, you will lose any finesse or control over your carving tools, and increase your chances of slipping. The carving instrument may cut into the wrong area of the carving, or worse yet, into you!

Try this handy, easy-to build bench hook

Carvers use a variety of means to secure their workpieces, but we like the convenience of a bench hook like the one shown *below*. By placing your carving on top of the plywood portion, you can carve in several directions before turning your workpiece around.

To build it, cut a piece of ¼" plywood to at least the dimensions

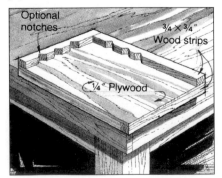

Optional notches
¾ × ¾" Wood strips
¼" Plywood

of your workpiece. Then, glue ¾x¾" wood strips along opposite corners on the top and bottom sides of the plywood. With a little more effort, you can add some notches, as shown in the illustration, allowing you to secure your carving in a greater number of directions.

Play it safe

You can minimize your chances of injury by following three rules: First, always push the carving tool away from you. If you're tempted to turn a blade toward yourself as you carve, instead take the time to reposition the carving. Second, keep both of your hands behind the cutting edge as you push it. Finally, take a good look at your tools before you pick them up. More than one carver has been cut by blindly reaching out for a tool, only to slice a finger by grabbing it by the blade.

Carve on the sapwood side

Before you trace a pattern onto a workpiece, examine the end grain. Since wood has a tendency to cup toward the heartwood, and toward its carved side, you can counteract these two forces and reduce the likelihood of the piece warping by carving on its sapwood side.

Sapwood side

Heartwood side

Don't carve too deep

Before you ever make your first cut, decide the maximum depth of the piece, and what areas you'll cut to that depth. Then, be careful not to cut any deeper—you'll find it practically impossible to disguise a cut that's too deep.

"It's a common myth that you need to carve deep, but good carvings achieve the illusion of depth while only going ⅜" or so deep," Jim said. "Look at any coin—there's an example of a very shallow relief carving that nevertheless has a good sense of depth."

How to carve in relief, photo-by-photo

Through the centuries, grape and leaf carvings have decorated everything from wine casks to furniture. The version *below* makes an ideal project for beginners because of its simple curves and classic beauty. In the process of making it, you'll learn many of the basic techniques of relief carving. To get started, you'll need the five carving tools and the bench hook described on *pages 33–34* along with a pattern, and a strop.

Your first steps: Lower the background

It's a relief carver's rule of thumb to "waste," or remove, the deepest portions of the design first. So we'll lower the background (everything outside the grape cluster) to ⅜"— the maximum depth for low-relief carvings. We show you how, starting with Step 1.

1. Carving tools tend to follow grain direction, so if you're not

careful, they can accidentally wander into your pattern. To keep this from happening, transfer arrows around the outside of the pattern as a reminder of the direction of your outlining cuts. As shown *below,* the arrows point in directions that will take your tools *away* from the pattern as they're pushed. Two-sided arrows indicate you can carve in either direction.

2. Use a V-tool, laid on its point, to make a ⅛"-deep groove around the perimeter of your pattern, staying about ¼" outside the pattern lines. Notice the comfortable, sitting position of the carver. Keep your strop nearby and place your chisels on a rag to protect their sharpened edges.

3. With a gouge, widen the groove to at least ½", still staying away from the pattern.

continued

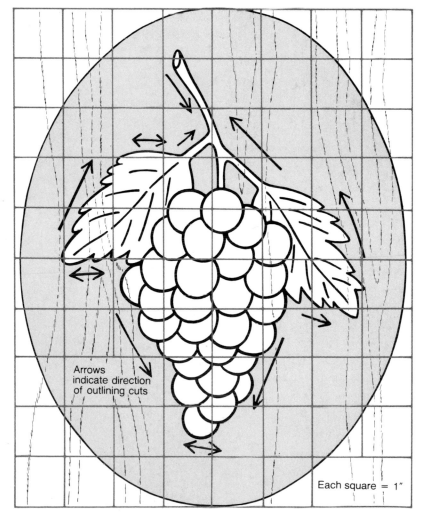

Arrows indicate direction of outlining cuts

Each square = 1"

STEP-BY-STEP RELIEF CARVING
continued

4. Now, lay the V-tool on its side and cut away stock up to, but not over, the outside pattern line. Skip the pockets along the leaves and grapes that are too tight to work into, and save those areas for later.

5. Remove material from tight areas along the outside of the grape cluster by first making a cross-grain stop cut with the V-tool on its side, ending the cut just short of the pattern line. Then, use the same tool and motion to remove the excess material by coming up to the first cut from the other side of the corner as shown *below.* You won't be able to remove the wood inside the serrated areas along the

leaves, so save those for later. Now, repeat Steps 3–5 until you've lowered the outline cut the full ⅜".

6. To remove stock from between the leaf serrations, first make stop cuts about ⅛" deep along both sides of the area. Start by plunging a knife into the tightest part of the corner, and pull the knife toward the outside of the pattern. To avoid breaking off leaf tips make the cross-grain cut first. Take your time, but if you accidentally break a leaf tip, don't worry—just modify the outside of the leaf. Your carving will look no worse for the breakage.

7. Remove the material between the two stop cuts by cutting into the tightest part of the corner with a skew chisel as shown *below.* Now, lift the waste wood out, and repeat this process while working toward the outside of the excess wood. Repeat Steps 6–7 until this area is flush with the surface along the outside of the pattern.

8. Next, remove the background material between the stems to a depth of ⅜". As you did in Step 6, first make stop cuts with a knife, along the outside of the pattern lines to a depth of ⅛", making sure the cuts connect in the corners, without crossing into the pattern. Take your time as you work along the stems; one stray cut could sever them completely.

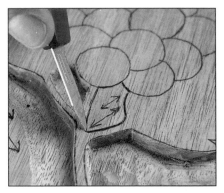

9. Use a skew chisel to remove the material between the stop cuts. Repeat Steps 8–9 until you've reached a depth of ⅜". As you near this depth, be careful not to cut too deep with your knife; the bottom of the hole should be smooth and free of cut marks.

10. Now, waste the background away with a gouge, working out from the first outline cuts toward the oval line surrounding the pattern. For these cuts, use a slightly exaggerated scooping

motion, plunging the gouge into the wood at about a 45–50° angle and laying it nearly flat as you take out 1"-long slices.

11. To shape the leaves, first define the edge between the grapes and leaves with a V-tool, just as you created the outline of the grapes against the background in Steps 2–5. This time, however, carve to a depth of only ⅛".

Then, use a straight chisel as shown *above*, to lower the leaves and give them a wavy appearance. We shaped one leaf so it sloped up to its middle from both sides, and the other so it sloped up in one direction from the grape side.

After completing the leaves, lower the stem about ⅛" and round it over with the straight chisel. Finally, cut the tip of the stem at an angle (see photo of finished piece on *page 35*) to make it appear clipped off by a grape picker.

12. Since grapes at the bottom of the cluster appear farthest from the eye perspectively, carve the bottom grapes first. Carve one grape at a time and work your way up the cluster. Outline the edge of each individual grape with a V-tool as shown *top center.*

13. Next, round over the edges of the grapes with a skew chisel. Notice that we've lowered the level

of the bottom-most grapes to enhance the design's sense of depth. As you work your way up the cluster, shape the grapes along the outside of the pattern first, making them just above the background and lower than the ones alongside them. You can achieve the illusion of globe-shaped grapes by rounding the edges of each grape and slanting its top surface downward into the grape above it.

14. To make leaf veins, first draw them in freehand with flowing lines, then lay the V-tool

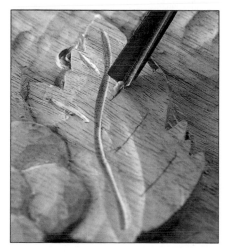

on its point, and make shallow incisions along the lines.

15. Finally, you'll need to "clean up" the loose shavings around the outside of the pattern and add to

the carving's illusion of depth with undercuts. Start by plunging a knife in at a slight inward angle and making short cuts along the pattern as shown *above.* Be careful to cut only as deep as the background.

16. With a straight chisel, remove the material you just cut in Step 15. Flatten the gouge tool marks closest to the pattern by gently scraping their ridges with a straight chisel.

Now, wipe mineral spirits over the carving to reveal any unwanted cut marks. Finish both sides of the piece immediately.

Buying Guide

• **Set of 6 carving tools.** This basic set contains the tools you'll need (plus two other gouges) for the project including a ¼" No. 9 gouge, ¼" No. 8 gouge, ⅜" No. 1 skew, ⅜" No. 5 gouge, ⅜" No. 1 chisel, and ¼" V-tool. Item No. 18A20. For current prices, contact Woodcraft Supply, 210 Wood County Industrial Park, P.O. Box 1686, Parkersburg, WV 26102, or call 800-225-1153.

• **Stanley Slimknife.** Available nationwide in many department stores and larger hardware stores.

DECORATIVE CARVING, SWISS STYLE

Wayne Barton was traveling light when he came to chip carve with the *WOOD*® magazine staff not long ago. That's because chip carving in the Swiss tradition calls for just two knives. They're the only tools he used to carve this beautiful weather station. Read on—we'll show you how to carve one yourself.

Sharp knives—the only way to carve

Chip carving with dull knives is like riding a bicycle with flat tires—you can do it, but it isn't very satisfying, and you have a hard time keeping control. "There is just no substitute for a sharp blade in carving," according to master carver Wayne Barton. So, before you try carving, put keen edges on those knives.

Sharpen both the cutting knife and stab knife on a medium ceramic stone and hone them on an ultra-fine one. For the cutting knife, lay the side of the blade on the stone and raise the back edge of the blade until you can just slip a dime under it. That's about 10°, the proper angle.

Sharpen the stab knife at the factory-set 30° angle. As you carve, touch up the edges occasionally on the ultra-fine stone.

Chip carving—cutting precise chips from wood to leave an engraved design—dates back to earliest civilizations. Swiss-style chip carving as practiced today has its roots in the Middle Ages.

Back then, peasants turned to *kerbschnitzen* (notch or groove carving) to embellish wooden furniture, utensils, and other household goods. Often, they decorated the home itself with carved doors and woodwork. Many designs reflected the intricate stone carving of the cathedrals.

Get a grip before you start

Professional chip-carver Wayne Barton uses the two Swiss-style knives illustrated *far right,* the *cutting* knife to remove wood and the *stab* knife to make decorative impressions. You'll do most of your work with the cutting knife, and you'll always hold it in one of two positions.

For the first position, hold the knife in your right hand (or left, if you're left-handed), placing the first joint of the thumb at the blade end of the handle. Then close your fingers around the handle. With the workpiece in your lap, turn the inside of your wrist toward your body, resting your thumb and index-finger knuckle on the wood as you cut.

For the second position, move your thumb to the spine of the blade, tilt the blade away from you, and rest your index finger knuckle on the wood. Compare the first and second positions in the illustrations *right.*

Maintain a 65° angle between the blade side and the workpiece in both positions. Keep your elbow close to your body when making straight or three-cornered chips, and make sure your knife hand rests on the work to help control your cuts.

Try out the basic cuts

You'll rely on three basic cuts for all of your chip carving—the straight chip (or straight line), the curved chip (or curved line), and the triangular chip. To begin cutting the straight chip, hold the knife in the first position, and cut along the pattern line in one direction. Then, turn the wood around and cut the other direction, releasing the chip. To vary chip size, change the cutting depth and the distance between your cuts, but don't change the angle of the blade to the work.

Cut the curved chip the same way, but raise the knife handle to reduce the length of the blade in the wood. For tighter-radius curves, raise the handle higher.

Carve the triangular chip in three steps (shown in the illustration *above*). Hold your knife in the first

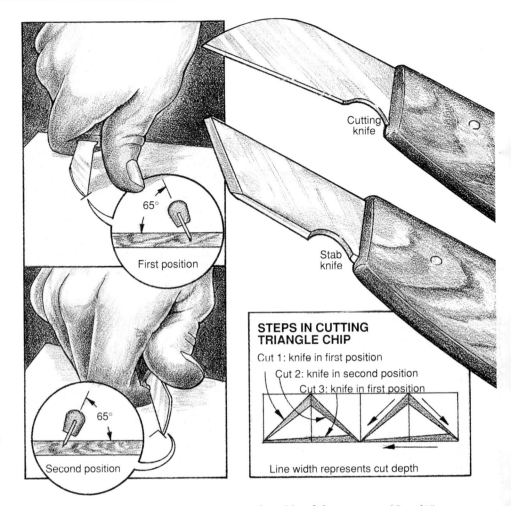

First position

Second position

STEPS IN CUTTING TRIANGLE CHIP

Cut 1: knife in first position
Cut 2: knife in second position
Cut 3: knife in first position

Line width represents cut depth

Cutting knife

Stab knife

position for the first cut. Rotate the wood about 90°, and change to the second grip position for the next cut. Without turning the board, go back to the first grip for the third cut.

The stab knife isn't a cutting knife, it makes decorative impressions. Grip it as you would an ice pick, keeping the sharp edge toward you as shown on *page 40,* Photo A. With the knife perpendicular to the workpiece, force the tip into the wood to make an indentation. Rock the knife toward you to extend the line.

Rout a carving board

Rout a decorative edge along both edges and ends of a ¾"-thick basswood board, leaving a 5⁵⁄₁₆x14⅝" carving face on top. To determine the initial board size, rout an edge on scrapwood and measure the width of the cut. Then, add twice that measurement to the length

and width of the pattern. (Our ⁵⁄₃₂" roman-ogee bit formed a profile ⅜" wide, so we added ¾" to each pattern dimension, and cut our carving board to 6⁵⁄₁₆x15⅜".)

Transfer the carving design to your board, following the instructions with the pattern, on *page 41.* Locate the center of the middle instrument hole at the center of your workpiece.

Let the chips fly!

Divide the carving into quarters, and then work from the outside in on each quarter. "Start with the largest chips in the area you're carving," Wayne advises. Carve the weather station's lace border beginning with the curved chips, followed by the diamonds and the small triangles. Then, carve the straight chips. Make the stab-knife impressions last.

"I like to start with cuts across the grain," Wayne says. As you progress, turn your work so you

continued

DECORATIVE CARVING, SWISS STYLE
continued

don't make the first cut along a new line toward work you've already done. If the wood splits out, apply a dab of glue with the knife tip to stick the flake back in.

Cut the curved lace border uniformly. Carve the chips shallow and narrow at each end and about ¹⁄₁₆–³⁄₃₂" wide at the middle (Photo B). Carve the straight border chips a little less than ¹⁄₁₆" wide. The constant knife angle maintains proper depth for both.

At each corner, carve four triangular chips to form a diamond inside a square. Then, cut a notch at the center of each side of the diamond to create the flower. Extend the large chips surrounding the instrument locations almost to the centerline on each side as shown in Photo C. Hold the standard knife angle as you cut the large chips. They'll be about ¼" deep.

Aim for uniformity among similar elements, but don't be dismayed if they don't match precisely. That's expected. "So what, if it's a little off," Wayne comments. "It's hand work."

Now, the weather report

Bore a ¼" pilot hole at the center of each instrument location with a brad-point bit in a drill press. Then, guide on the pilot hole to bore each instrument hole with a hole-saw. The Klockit instruments we used mount in 2⁵⁄₁₆" holes.

Now, erase any leftover layout marks and sand the carving lightly, but don't sand away any of the sharp edges. Apply dull or matte-finish polyurethane with light spray applications from several angles. After the finish dries, mount the instruments and hang the board for all to see.

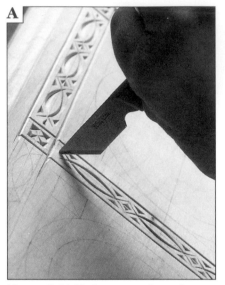

The stab knife leaves a triangular impression when forced straight into the wood.

Supplies

Stock: Basswood ¾x6½x15½". Tools: Swiss chip-carving knives: cutting knife, stab knife; Layout tools: compass, metric ruler; Ceramic sharpening stones: medium, ultra-fine; Spray-on polyurethane finish.

Buying Guide

• **Complete chip-carving kit.** Swiss-made cutting knife and stab knife; medium and ultra-fine ceramic sharpening stones; book, *Chip Carving Techniques and Patterns* by Wayne Barton; metric ruler; compass for layout; and two basswood practice boards. For current prices, contact Alpine School of Woodcarving, Ltd., 225 Vine Ave., Park Ridge, IL 60068.

• **Cutting knife and stab knife.** Knives only. For current prices, contact address *above*.

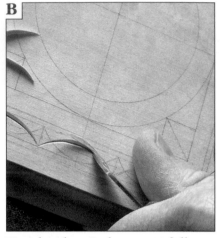

Your hand can't always rest fully on the board, but you can maintain control with your thumb on the surface, as here in cutting curved chips for the border near the edge of the board.

The cutting knife remains at a constant 65° side angle to the work As a result, large, wide chips, such as those around instrument holes, will be deeper than the small ones in the border.

• **Weather instruments**. Thermometer, hygrometer, and barometer, product No. 71103. For current prices, contact Klockit, Box 636, Lake Geneva, WI 53147, or call 800-556-2548.

Template

Straight chip   Curved chip

Stab-knife impression   Triangular chip

4mm

Blue lines for
layout only —
Do not carve

**FULL-SIZED
PARTIAL
PATTERN**

2mm

7mm

Radius to fit
instrument

For a full-sized
pattern, photocopy
the section *left* twice.
Designate one copy
the center. Cut the
other copy in half at
the middle instru-
ment's horizontal
centerline. Align the
cut edge of the top
piece with the top
instrument centerline
on the uncut copy.
Join the bottom half to
the uncut copy at the
lower instrument's
centerline. Tape them
together, and cut off
the top and bottom
outside the border.
    Trace the pattern
onto your board with
graphite paper. Or,
lay out the lines
shown on the pattern
and draw the design
with a soft pencil.
Transfer the template
to stiff cardboard to
aid in tracing or
drawing the curved
border.

41

CARVE A COLORFUL FEATHER PIN

If carving an entire bird seems too much to tackle, just do part of one—a feather. Harold Rosauer, *below,* a Manchester, Iowa, teacher and carver, often takes a break from birds to carve lifelike feathers that he makes into pins. We visited him recently to find out how to carve one of his favorites, a wood duck feather.

Trace the full-sized pattern *below* onto your wood, and cut out the blank with a bandsaw or scrollsaw. Draw the quill line with a pencil.

On each edge of the cutout, draw a line that starts from the top side at the rounded feather tip, curves down to the bottom at the widest part of the the blank, and then curves back up to the middle of the edge at the base of the feather (shown *below right*). From there, draw the line straight along the quill to the end.

Now, rev up your carver

A flexible-shaft machine, such as the Foredom, fitted with a structured tungsten-carbide burr ¾" in diameter, as shown in the photos, makes quick work of carving the feather to

shape. But if this is your first whirl with power carving, try a less aggressive tool. A good choice: a hand-held rotary tool (such as Dremel's Moto-Tool) equipped with a bullet-shaped carbide or ruby carving bit about ¼" diameter. (Most hobby shops and many hardware stores sell such bits.) You also can carve the feather with hand tools.

Hold the power carver as you would hold a knife, and draw the

**FULL-SIZED PATTERN
WOOD DUCK FEATHER**

Base
Quill
Woodburn lines
Tip
Carve slight relief in shaded area to create wavy end

rotary cutter along the surface *(opposite, top right).* Remove a small amount of wood with each pass.

Form a curve from the middle of the feather to the line drawn on each edge (*opposite, middle right*).

Now, the carving will resemble a lens shape when viewed from the end. Hollow out a slight relief in the area on the right side of the quill line, creating a wave on the end, shown *opposite, top left.* Carve the hollow about ⅟₁₆" deep at the

Draw the curved edge line and the quill line on the blank. The quill line ends just short of the notch at the feather tip.

tip. Next, carve the underside of the end to match the top contour as shown *opposite, lower right.*

Thin the end to ⅟₁₆" or less for a light, wind-rippled look. Taper the hollow to a flat surface about midway down the feather.

Then, turn the feather over, and carve the quill. From the top surface, cut down to the line on the edge of the quill, creating a square stem from the base out to the end of the quill.

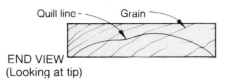

Quill line · Grain

END VIEW
(Looking at tip)

Grind away the resulting hump near the base at the center of the feather.

Change to a sanding drum to round the quill to about ⅛" diameter. Take care—it's easy to break the quill off or make it too thin. Round over the edges as you hand-sand both sides of the feather. Then, redraw the quill line.

Burn in feathery features

For extra realism, detail the feather with a woodburning tool. Otherwise, skip down to the next section to paint your feather.

Using a flat tip as shown *below* or the side of the tip on your woodburning pen, burn a slight depression along each side of the quill line. The quill should describe a graceful arc, tapering from the approximate width of the carved quill at the base to that of a sharp pencil line at the tip. Accentuate the taper by burning deeper at the base of the feather than at the tip. Blend the burned area into the surface.

Raise the quill on the feather by depressing the wood on either side of the quill line with a woodburner.

Then, texture the feather with parallel lines. A density of about 45 lines per inch looks realistic. (You may have to sharpen your wood-burner tip on a stone to make such fine lines.)

From the burned area next to the quill, extend slightly curved lines to the feather's edge. Angle them upward at about 30° from the quill (see photo at *right*).

Don't worry about burning continuous lines from center to edge, but concentrate on keeping

Grip the power carver as you would a knife, supporting the workpiece with your thumb. Pare away wood from the center of the blank toward the edge. Remove wood in a series of light cuts.

The top surface curves down to the guideline on the edge. Underside at tip will be cut away to the bottom of the line.

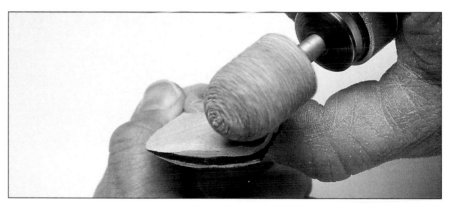

Carve the underside of the feather to match the top contour. Make the end thin for a light, natural look. Back is nearly flat at the bottom of the feather.

them parallel. Burn sharp lines about the color of burnt toast.

Burn 6–10 randomly located splits through the edge of the feather. Let the woodburner tip burn through the wood as shown on *page 44, top*. Vary the width and length of the splits.

Paint a pretty plume

Seal the woodburned surface with a sanding sealer (Harold uses Benjamin Moore Quick-Dry Sanding Sealer), and then prime it *continued*

Starting in the depression beside the quill, woodburn slightly curved texture lines to the edges. Keep them parallel.

CARVE A COLORFUL FEATHER PIN
continued

with a thin coat of acrylic gesso. Paint the feather with acrylic artist's colors (listed on *page 45*) and a medium brush (a No. 5 works well). Squeeze out a bit of each color (blobs the size of pencil erasers will do) onto a damp plate or palette. Thin the paints with a few drops of water.

Mix small amounts of the two yellows to match the color shown *below right*. (Don't fret over it; close will be good enough.) Paint the front of the feather, and then clean your brush in water.

With the yellow still wet, apply medium gray over the lower third of the feather. Clean the brush again, pat it until almost dry on a paper towel, and then brush across the yellow/gray division in both directions to blend the colors as shown *right*. Now, your feather should be bright yellow at the top, grayish yellow just below the middle, and gray at the base.

Let the paint dry (you can help it along with a hair dryer), and paint the feather the same way again. After this base coat dries, paint the tip black. Bring the black down about ³⁄₁₆" from the tip at the center, curving the lower line downward from the center to the edges. As you paint, remember that slightly wavering lines with fuzzy edges will look more authentic than straight ones with sharp edges.

Let it dry, and then paint a ³⁄₁₆"-wide white band beneath the black one, paralleling the curvature of the black. After that dries, paint another black stripe about ¹⁄₁₆" wide, and then a ¹⁄₁₆" white stripe, as shown in the photo *opposite top left*. Let dry, and then put a second coat on all of the stripes.

To reduce the time you spend waiting for paint to dry, combine steps. Paint the black top and the

Burn through the edge in several random spots to create splits. Vary the length and width of the spots for realism.

Paint the feather bright yellow. While the yellow is still wet, paint the lower part medium gray, blending the gray into the yellow.

first white stripe as above. Then, when you paint the next black stripe, recoat the black on top at the same time. Continue in this fashion until you've put two coats on all of the stripes.

Don't be concerned if some of the white bleeds along the woodburned lines into the black areas. This will soften the lines, making your feather more true-to-life. Thin a small amount of

raw sienna to a watery consistency, and paint a narrow stripe on each side of the quill on the yellow portion of the feather. Blend it outward with a damp brush until only a hint of the color remains, creating a slight, reddish brown highlight along either side of the quill.

If you didn't woodburn your feather, dry-brush a few random black streaks through the yellow

Uneven lines look more natural when painting stripes on the feather. Thinned paints won't clog woodburned texture lines.

Vermiculation creates a pattern on the feather. Paint the broken lines by applying small, closely spaced dots.

area. Pat the dry brush on the surface of unthinned black paint to pick up a little pigment, and then lightly brush a few barely visible lines across the feather's surface.

Now, for some vermiculation

Vermiculation, the pattern of wavy lines on the feather, consists of closely spaced dots applied with a small, pointed brush (No. 0, for example). Start with a row of black dots along the line where the bottom white stripe meets the yellow. Avoid uniform, evenly spaced, and neatly aligned dots—you want a ruffled appearance.

Paint four or five rows on one half of the feather, spacing them about ¹⁄₁₆" apart, and then paint the corresponding rows on the other

side of the quill, as shown *above right*. You should have room for about 20 lines of vermiculation on the feather.

About halfway down, start adding a bit of gray to your black paint, using a little more gray as you near the base of the feather. When you're done, go back and dab a spot of gray on a dozen or so randomly selected dots.

Then, accent the splits with black paint, and add a few black strokes to simulate internal splits, shown *below left*. If you didn't woodburn any splits, paint them with a black line starting at the edge. (The feather on the *right* in the photo wasn't woodburned.)

Paint the quill and the raised quill line titanium white. Don't paint the line all the way to the top of the feather, let it fade out ¹⁄₁₆–¹⁄₃₂" shy of

the end. Let the white dry, and then apply iridescent white. Attach a bar pin (available from craft suppliers) lengthwise on the flat part of the back with epoxy glue.

Supplies
Stock: ⅜×2×3" basswood or other carving wood. Tools: Flexible-shaft machine or hand-held rotary tool; carbide or ruby carving bits, ¼" diameter, coarse and fine; structured tungsten carbide burr, ½" or ¾" diameter; sanding drum for power carver; woodburning tool (optional). Finishing Supplies: Sanding sealer; acrylic gesso; acrylic artist's colors: Iridescent white, Titanium white, Turner's yellow (yellow ochre), Medium yellow, Neutral gray, Raw sienna, Black; Brushes: Round No. 5, No. 0.

Feathers look good whether woodburned (*left*) or not (*right*).

WHITTLING

Roald Tweet whittles a bird while visiting the *WOOD*® magazine shop.

In this hurry-up, fast-paced world of ours, it's nice to know that some things never change. Take whittling, for example. People have been having fun with this simple type of woodworking for lots of years—and for lots of good reasons. It's relaxing, easy to do, and oh, so satisfying. Come on and give it a try. You'll be glad you did.

"Whittling is meaningless," Roald Tweet, *above*, maintains. And that's exactly what he loves about it.

A professor of English and composition at Augustana College in Rock Island, Illinois, he spends much of his day immersed in "meaning." To unwind, Roald picks up a stick and a knife, and makes chips. It's pure relaxation.

Nothing else in woodworking demands so little yet returns so much. A whittler isn't obligated to produce useful items—a little ornament or figure is enough. And a whittler doesn't need a shop or a workbench—a porch step works just fine. When you come down to it, all a whittler really needs are a knife, a piece of wood, and a little bit of free time.

1. Pare away wood quickly for roughing with this basic whittling stroke.

Whittling off the woodpile

The wood Roald likes to whittle would be mere kindling to most people. He whittles what he finds—twigs and small branches.

"Since the growth rings are so close together in a small branch, the grain is dramatic," he explains. "Part of the fun, too, is that you discover the most interesting woods—woods you wouldn't ordinarily use."

The whittling prof likes lilac for its subtle grain. And he enjoys cutting into magnolia and catalpa just because they're unusual. Actually, Roald will try anything. His favorite? Cherry.

Get yourself a sharp knife

Roald likes the long handle and short, stout blade of a standard bench-type carving knife for whittling. But any knife (even a pocketknife) with a sharp, sturdy blade and a handle that affords a good grip will do.

Don't use a dull knife. Accidents happen when you try to force a

2. Push the blade with your thumb for a powerful, controlled cutting stroke as shown *above*.

3. Use the paring cut for smoothing the surface or whittling details. Let the workpiece shield your thumb.

blunt blade through wood. As for handling the knife, anybody who has ever picked one up to do more than spread peanut butter probably knows the three basic whittling cuts instinctively.

• For rough-shaping, hold the stick in your left hand and the knife in your right (assuming you're right-handed), as shown in Photo 1 *above left*. Push the knife downward and away from you, the way you did when you made pointed sticks as a kid.

• For finer shaping, make shorter cuts. Control the knife with your right hand, but push the blade with your left thumb as shown in Photo 2.

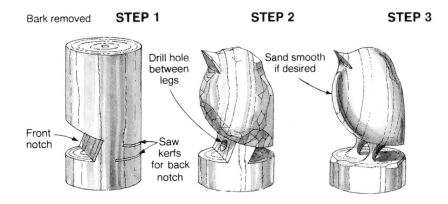

Bark removed **STEP 1**   **STEP 2**   **STEP 3**

Drill hole between legs

Front notch

Saw kerfs for back notch

Sand smooth if desired

• For details or surface smoothing, switch to the paring cut shown in Photo 3. Place your right thumb at the top of the cut. Then, close your hand to pull the knife toward your thumb. Use this cut for maximum control.

Birds, whimmydiddles, and lots more

Roald doesn't give much thought to what he'll whittle. As often as not, he makes a bird. (His birds, full-sized drawings shown *below,* are well known around the Augustana campus.) But, it could just as easily be a letter opener, weed pot, spoon, chain, whimmydiddle, or toothpick.

A whimmydiddle? You've probably seen one. That's the folk toy with 8 or 10 notches whittled along a stick. A smaller twig nailed to one end like a propeller spins whenever someone rubs another stick along the notches.

Whatever you decide to whittle, keep it simple. Avoid highly detailed forms. "Whittling should be relaxing. Don't concentrate too much on it, and don't worry about a pattern. Sketch some simple guidelines, and then just follow the wood," Roald says as he rounds one end of a branch for the top of a bird's head. "See how the color changes here?" he

asks, pointing to a hood shape formed where he has whittled down to the darker heartwood. "That will set off the head."

Rough out thin or fragile parts, such as a bird's legs, as you whittle, but save completing them for last. You can rely entirely on your knife or, like Roald, you can take advantage of other tools. He saws notches (shown *left,* Step 1) and drills out wood (Step 2) when forming legs for his birds, for example.

If you've whittled a keeper, burnish it by rubbing the surface with another piece of wood. (If you prefer a smooth surface, sand it first.) Roald finishes his pieces with clear rubbing oil.

Otherwise, just remember this: There are no bad whittlings, only small pieces of firewood.

FULL-SIZED PATTERNS

FULL-SIZED DRAWINGS

FRONT   SIDE

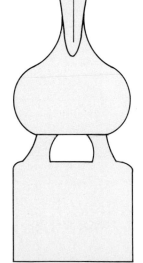

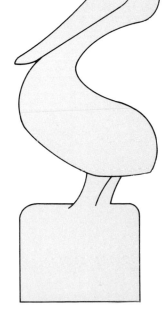

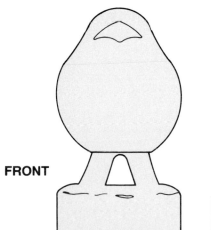

FRONT

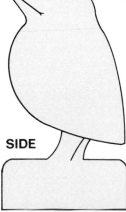

SIDE

MAKING FACES

There's no need to get flustered when its time to put a face on your carving. With the right proportions and some simple techniques, you can't go wrong. As a bonus, we'll show you great ways to make the eyes—often the most troublesome step in face carving.

Proportion is everything

To carve a human face, you must know what one looks like. Sure, you've seen a lot of faces, but have you studied them? Let's study the nearest face—your own.

With your thumb on your chin bring the index finger to the tip of your nose. Hold the measurement and move your hand so the thumb rests on your nose. Your index finger should fall close to your eyebrows. Still holding the measurement, place your thumb on an eyebrow and notice that your index finger hits near the top of your forehead. Not precisely, but pretty close. *Discovery No. 1: The nose and eyebrows divide the face into thirds.*

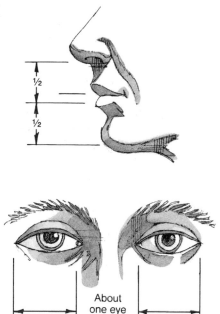

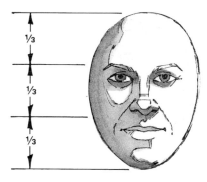

Now, put your thumb back on your chin and bring your index finger to your lips. Move your thumb to your lips and you should end up with your finger a little above the tip of your nose. *Discovery No. 2: The mouth sits a little higher than halfway between the chin and nose.*

Next, measure the width of one eye with your thumb-and-finger calipers. Now, when you move your thumb to the inside corner of one eye, your index finger will fall neatly into the inside corner of the other one. *Discovery No. 3: The eyes are about one eyewidth apart.*

About one eye width apart

Okay, here's another one. Point your index finger straight up from one corner of your mouth. You'll notice that you can't see much that's directly in front of you with the eye on that side since the finger goes right across the middle of it. Try it on the other side. *Discovery No. 4: Vertical lines through the pupils mark the sides of the mouth.*

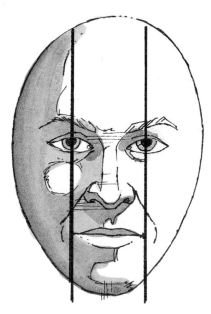

Press your hand to your forehead horizontally (as if intense study has given you a headache) and then to the lower part of your face,

covering your mouth. When you lift your hand away each time, you'll see that it is bent. *Discovery No. 5: The face curves at the top and bottom, and along the sides. It isn't flat.*

The face doesn't just sit on front of the head, it wraps around it. "A bird's-eye view of a human head suggests an egg shape, or home plate on a baseball diamond," WOOD® magazine's carving consultant Harley Refsal explains. The greatest width spans the tops of the ears, and the longest distance is from the back of the head the tip of the nose. "If the head on your carving is not shaped this way, your completed face may look convincing when viewed from the front, but you will not be able to see facial features when viewing a profile," he notes.

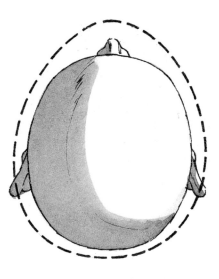

To get the correct wraparound look, Harley starts carving a face on a corner of his workpiece. On a full-figure carving with a rectangular head, he carves the front of the head to a corner before beginning the face.

Let's try it

Grab a piece of carving wood (basswood does nicely) about 1×1×8", a sharp carving knife, and a pencil, and we'll craft a face in five easy steps. Turn a corner of your workpiece toward you, and then cut three sawtooth notches
continued

MAKING FACES
continued

about ¾" apart along the edge, Step 1. The points will become the brow, nose, and chin.

Next, pencil in the smile lines, starting from the sides of the nose. Extend them downward and outward like the legs of the letter A, Step 2. Carve the smile lines with V-cuts. Form the mouth with a horizontal V-cut just above the midpoint between the nose and chin. Cut between the smile lines, but don't connect with them. Create the lower lip with a slightly wider V-cut just below and parallel to the mouth, Step 3.

Add eye sockets to complete the basic face shape. Form them with wide, shallow, horizontal V-cuts, one on each side of the nose, Step 4. Place the bottom of the cut near the tip of the nose and the top near the eyebrows. As well as establishing eye locations, these cuts give the nose a basic shape.

And now, for the eyes

If eyes are the windows of the soul, then it's the eyes that bring a little bit of soul to any human-face sculpture. You may be able to get away with a lumpy nose or too-thin lips on your carving. But, beady little eyes set too close together will make what you wanted to be a kindly old codger look like some demented character out of a Stephen King novel.

Your first step toward pleasing eyes is to place a pencil mark in each eye socket, straight up from the corners of the mouth. Next, draw a line centered on the mark. It sets the width of the eye, so don't make it too short. Widths vary—sometimes an eye is nearly as wide as the mouth.

For starters, make your eye lines about one-half to two-thirds the mouth's width. Adjust your eye width until it looks right for the

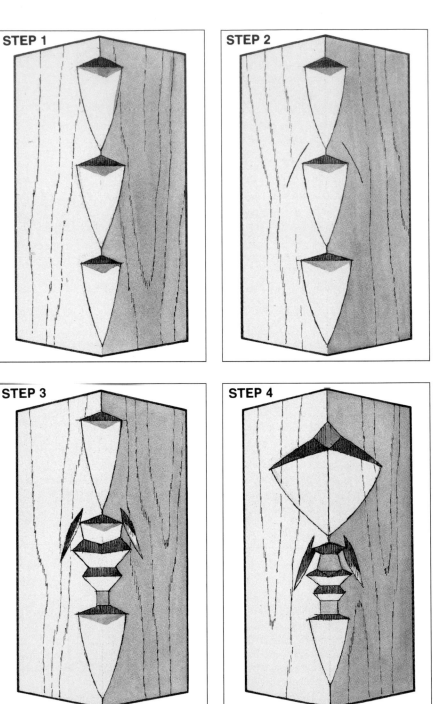

character you're creating. Space the eyes about an eye-width apart.

A low, wide triangle located at the V of the eye socket makes a

simple and effective eye treatment, particularly for flat-plane or other less detailed carvings. Let's add this stylized variety to your practice

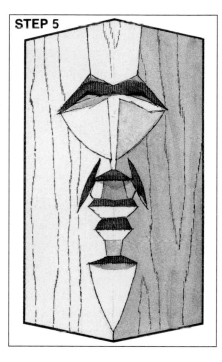

STEP 5

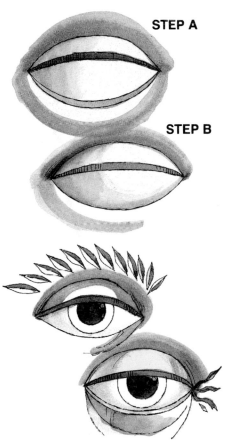

STEP A

STEP B

carving knives work great for fine wrinkles.

Form eyebrows with a series of fine, random V-cuts. Woodburn eyebrows for greater detail. Woodburning creates fine wrinkles or creases, too.

Try changing character by changing the line across the carved, oval eye described above. Raising the line to reveal more of the pupil and iris will, of course, give a wide-eyed look—possibly surprise, shock, innocence. Lowering the line will result in a range of expressions from sleepy to downright sinister.

Practice makes perfect

You can carve any style face with these basic proportions and techniques. For a more realistic carving, soften the exaggerated lines and angular planes. For caricatures, accentuate the features.

You can master faces if you keep studying and carving them. Make faces into a mirror (be sure you've shut the bathroom door before you start this) to see what happens to your mouth, nose, eyes, and brow. Study newspaper and magazine photographs of people, resin study casts (available from woodcarving suppliers), and other carvings. Carve a child's face (smooth, soft curves) and an old cowboy (wrinkled, angular). Carve a woman's face. You'll end up with a lot of totem poles, but you'll also be able to put a better face forward with your carvings.

face, concentrating for now on size and location.

Lay out the eye location as described earlier. Now, cut the straight line with the tip of your knife. Then, cut upward from each end to form the triangle. Place the triangle's tip at the pencil mark you drew, where the pupil would be, Step 5.

To carve a more detailed eye, start with placement as previously described. Then, instead of making a triangle, draw an elongated oval (picture a long, narrow football) with a slightly curved horizontal line across the middle. Set the eye width with the horizontal line; draw the oval about half as high as it is wide, Step A, *above right*. Stop-cut the outline and carve a relief in the eye socket around the oval. Next, cut the horizontal line and carve the bottom half slightly lower to form an eyeball under the eyelid. Round-over the edges to blend the eye into the face, as shown in Step B.

Now, you can carve a partial circle on the lower part of the oval eye to represent the pupil and iris, or you can paint them for greater detail. If you intend to paint your carving, follow the steps shown *above* to put some twinkle into the eyes. If painting an oval eye, paint the top line along the eyelid, and the color highlights onto the carved oval. Watercolors or thinned acrylics work great, adding color without covering up carved details.

Add some character

Extra details, such as wrinkles, crow's-feet, or bags under the eyes, add realism and make your carving more interesting. Pencil in these details first, trying different effects, and then carve them with your knife tip or a small V-tool. Chip-

BARKROSING

You won't find an easier way then barkrosing to dress up anything wooden. With a knife, some sandpaper, and a chunk of bark, you have what it takes to make a plain object look like an old-world treasure.

"Anybody can do barkrosing," says woodcarver Harley Refsal as we sit at his dining room table, etching patterns into pieces of wood. He's right; it's easy. And it's a great embellishment for almost anything wooden.

Barkrosing, coloring a knife-cut design with tree bark, originated in Norway centuries ago. Historians don't know precisely when, however. That's partly due to its humble beginnings.

"This wasn't fine art," explains Harley, *WOOD*® magazine's carving consultant. "It was decoration for everyday items. Such things were used until they wore out, then were thrown away. So, they never made it into museums for study."

Despite being a carved decoration, barkrosing leaves a smooth surface, an advantage for at least two common early-day uses. Kitchenware, such as bowls and spoons, wiped clean easily. And on skis, barkrosing didn't collect snow and ice as raised carving or open engraving would have.

An adaptable adornment

Today, barkrosing still fills the bill for quick, easy-to-do decoration on utilitarian wooden objects. "It's a great way to make a nice, quick, handmade gift," Harley points out. "Just buy a plain wooden spoon and dress it up with a little barkrosing."

To try out that idea, we head downtown in Harley's hometown, Decorah, Iowa. There, a quick search nets a wooden spoon with a plain, flat handle. Follow along now

A

Draw light guidelines. That way, they'll come off without excessive sanding. Too much sanding to remove the guidelines after you've cut your design into the wood will ruin your work. Try out your design first on paper.

as Harley transforms it from ordinary into distinctive in a few easy steps.

Pencil a few doodles

The first step is to draw a design onto the handle. "A simple geometric pattern looks good and follows tradition," Harley explains. "But, you could do monograms or designs as fancy as you dare."

"When in doubt," he suggests, "draw two parallel lines as a border, and crosshatch between them. Diamonds make a nice ornament." (See the samples *below right* and *opposite*.) He decides on a crosshatched border and stacked diamonds for our spoon.

Harley sketches the major elements onto the spoon handle, as shown in photo A. He doesn't draw in all of the details–just indications where they will go. "You can follow a fine line better with the knife blade, so use a sharp pencil," he advises.

Engrave those fine lines

Next, he inscribes the design. "Any sharp knife will suffice, but the closer to

B

Hold the knife as close to the tip as possible for maximum control. Be sure to use a sharp knife for clean, crisp lines.

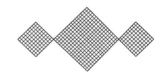

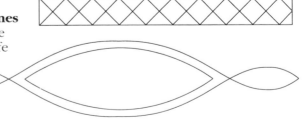

C

A piece of 180-grit sandpaper produces fine bark dust in a hurry. We show walnut here, but other tree barks will work.

D

Rub the bark powder into the lines with your fingertips. This really isn't as messy as it looks, but do it over paper anyway.

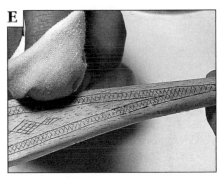

E

Salad-bowl oil brings out the color of the barkrosing, and soaks into the powdered bark to bind it to the base wood. You also could apply lacquer or polyurethane for a protective coating on decorative items.

F

Harley Refsal used the 6mm Swiss knife blank shown to carve the design into the spoon handle. Any knife you can grip near the tip will work.

the tip you can grip it, the better," Harley says. He uses a 6mm Swiss knife blank (Catalog No. 05S12 from Wood-craft Supply Co., 800-225-1153), but you may find an X-acto knife more comfortable to use because of its thicker grip.

The technique is simple: Just grip the knife as you would a pencil, and score along guidelines, shown in Photo B. A simple incision with the knife perpendicular to the surface works best.

Harley presses the knife tip into the wood just deeply enough to open a visible slit. "For bolder lines, cut a little deeper and wider," he says, "but keep each line uniform." Pay attention to the grain

lest it steer your knife off into a direction you weren't planning to go. Erasing a mistake, when it's possible, calls for a lot of sanding.

Now, Harley grabs a chunk of walnut bark scavenged from his yard. He rubs the corky outside of the bark along a piece of 180-grit sandpaper, making fine, brown dust (Photo C).

You can combine elements from traditional designs such as the ones around these pages to make borders and ornaments. Any geometric designs, old or new, adapt well to the technique.

Go ahead, rub it in

Then, he picks up a pinch of the bark powder and rubs it into the incised design with his fingertips (Photo D). He works bark dust into all parts of the design. Next, he lightly sands the carved and filled area with 400-grit sandpaper to remove the edges raised by the blade.

Finally, he applies a clear oil finish (Photo E). For the spoon, which could be used for serving or preparing food, he uses Behlen's Salad Bowl Oil.

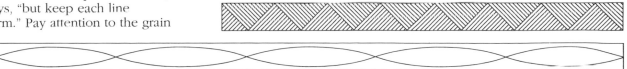

CARVING PROJECTS

In this section we've gathered a group of projects sure to please every carver—no matter what level of skill. Here you'll find an array of subjects from nature and items that will serve and decorate your home for years to come.

CARVER'S-PRIDE TRADE SIGN

Whether you're a veteran carver or a newcomer, here's a powerful statement you can make in wood. A dynamic portrayal of a woodcarver, low-relief lettering, and your name all work together to instantly identify you as one who cares about carving.

For centuries craftsmen and tradesmen have announced their shops with distinctive pictorial signs. Years ago, many people couldn't read, but they could quickly recognize a barber pole or giant pair of glasses.

Today, graphic signs stand out on a crowded street and are easy to recognize. Attractive, finely crafted signs proclaim: "I am proud of what I do, and I do it well." Knowing that you carvers feel that way, we asked Robert Thomas, Jr., a woodcarver and graphic artist, to design this one especially for you.

Personalize your pattern

First, photocopy the half-sized pattern *below* at 100 percent. Then, place your name in the space provided at the bottom. Carefully hand-letter your name in block letters to match the sign style. Or, you can buy rub-on letters from a stationery or art supply store for a professional look. In the Letratype rub-on line of 36-point (½"-tall) type (see the Buying Guide on *page 57* for our source), try Clarendon Medium for names 12–15 letters long, Times Bold for longer names, or Clarendon Bold for shorter ones.

Remember, you also can adjust the size of the space for the name,

if necessary. After all, this will be your sign.

Next, lay the pattern down

Now, enlarge your personalized, half-sized pattern on a photocopying machine set at 200 percent. The enlarged pattern barely fits one 11x17" sheet of paper, so enlarge it in two halves and tape them together. If the copier doesn't go up to 200 percent, enlarge the pattern at 141 percent and then enlarge the resulting copy at 141 percent. (Or, use 121 percent, 129 percent, and 129 percent.)

Place the enlargement, with transfer paper underneath, on the sapwood side of your workpiece (the tops of the end-grain arcs point to the sapwood side). Tape the *continued*

HALF-SIZED PATTERN

WOODCARVING

Texture with gouge

Texture with gouge

35°

FULL-SIZED DEPTH GAUGE

COLOR KEY

Original surface

⅛"

3/16"

5/16"

⅜"

½"

BY

(Your name goes here)

CARVER'S-PRIDE TRADE SIGN
continued

pattern in place, and then trace all the lines except for the slanted, parallel lines in the background. (A French curve and ruler will add to your accuracy.)

Remove the paper pattern and spray artist's fixative or clear lacquer onto the carving blank so you won't smear the lines as you carve. Then, bandsaw around the sign perimeter. Saw slightly outside the pattern line, and sand down to it.

Now, make some chips

Start carving the central design. Hold your carving in place with a bench hook or, for more convenience, a urethane mat.

With your bench knife, make vertical cuts along the pattern lines, as shown *right*. These *stopcuts* enable you to cut toward a line without removing wood beyond it—they stop your cut. You can stop-cut with your V-tool, too, by cutting along the pattern line with one edge of the tool held vertically. Whichever tool you use, take care not to undercut the line. Straight, vertical sides will make your sign look sharp.

Transfer the depth gauge on the *previous page* to a ½x2½" strip cut from a file card or old business card. Then, start removing wood with your gouges to establish the relief levels, a process called *grounding*.

Choose the tools you're most comfortable with for grounding (We prefer palm-handled tools for ease of control.) At various times, you'll use gouges, skew chisels, V-tools, and your knife. Some carvers like spoon-bent gouges for relief work, but you can complete this carving without them.

As you carve, measure the depth with the gauge and a straightedge as shown *right*. Work down to the final levels in stages, alternately stop-cutting and removing wood. Don't try to do it in one cut, and don't concentrate on a single area. Rather, carve the entire design as one piece.

Create straight sides for your relief areas by stop-cutting along pattern lines. Be careful not to slope or undercut the sides.

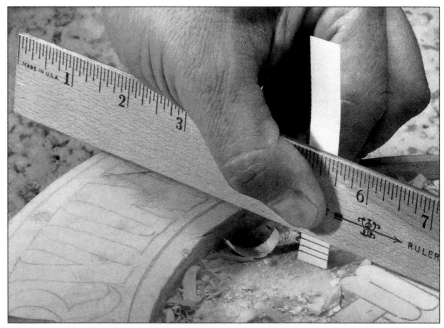

Check carving levels with the depth gauge, which is keyed to the color-coded pattern. Measure each level at several points.

As you approach the final depths indicated by the pattern color tints and gauge, start to smooth the relief surfaces. But, don't aim for the glassy smoothness of a tabletop. Rather, give your sign character by letting some tool marks and texture show that it's handwork.

Take care of a few details

With the grounding completed, draw lines ¼" apart at a 35° angle where shown on the pattern. With each line as a center, dig the flutes about ⅛" deep with a 5mm No. 9 gouge as shown *below*. Then, carve a narrow groove in the bottom of each with a 1mm U-veiner. Round the top corners with the skew.

Separate the fingers on the hand holding the chisel with the 1mm U-veiner. Then, with your bench knife, contour the chip at the chisel tip as shown on the pattern and in

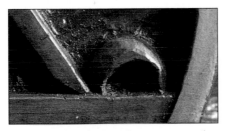

Contour the chip to form a smooth curl. For the best effect match the slope angle on the inside right end with that on the outside left end.

the photo, *bottom*. Round the chisel handle with a skew, and then chamfer each corner of the blade and each finger slightly.

Separate the carver's mallet arm from the sleeve with a shallow V-tool or veiner groove. Then, with your knife, pare the thumb down so it's a little lower than the mallet handle. Chamfer the arm and hand, sleeves, and body with the skew. Sand the corners of the mallet and the carver's workpiece just enough to smooth them.

Begin texturing the background with a deep gouge, carving along the pattern line. Then, groove the bottom of each cut with a U-veiner. The pattern shows the 35° angle to use for laying out the lines.

Contour the chip to form a smooth curl. For the best effect, match the slope angle on the inside right end with that on the outside left end.

Put it in writing

Stop-cut the lettering, being particularly careful to maintain straight, vertical lines and smooth curves (a V-tool works well for this). For curves, try stop-cutting with a gouge of appropriate curvature (*sweep*) held vertically.

Carve only a shallow relief around the letters (⅛" on your depth gauge). Because of the

shallow relief, you won't make many cuts before reaching final depth, reducing the number of opportunities to correct wavy lines. So, start slightly outside the carving line with your first cut and work deliberately toward it.

A worthy finish

Apply a dark stain to your sign (we used Minwax Early American). For a rich look, stain it once, let that coat dry, and then stain it again. After the stain has dried, paint the letters with country red acrylic artist's paint. Accent the border with antique beige. When the paint has dried, apply two coats of satin polyurethane varnish.

Supplies

Wood: 1½x12x15" basswood or other carving wood; Tools: Gouges: 10mm No. 7, 8mm No.1, 8mm No.1 bent, 8mm No.5, 6mm No.7, 5mm No.9, 3mm No.11 U-veiner, 1mm No.11 U-veiner; V-tools: 3mm No. 12, 3mm No. 12 bent; Skew; 8mm No. 2; Knife: Bench knife.

Note: Further information on the carving tools listed above can be found on pages 5–6.

Buying Guide

• **Bandsawed blank in northern basswood.** For current prices, contact Ozark Mountain Crafts, Box R, Branson, MO 65616, or call 417-561-8275.

• **Rub-on letters.** Letratype capitals and lower-case, 36 point, in Clarendon Medium (46249CLN), Times Bold (48129CLN), or Clarendon Bold (96916CLN). For current prices, contact The Art Store, 600 Harding Road, Des Moines, IA 50312, or call 800-652-2225.

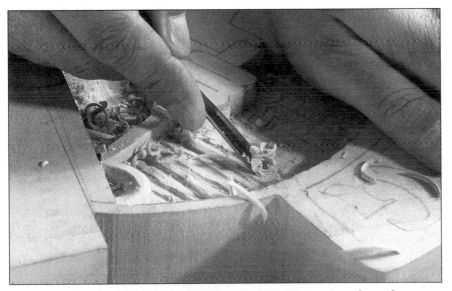

Begin texturing the background with a deep gouge, carving along the pattern line. Then, groove the bottom of each cut with a U-veiner. The pattern shows the 35° angle to use for laying out the lines.

CARVE SHALAKO: A KACHINA-STYLE PENDANT

Designed by Kansas City carver Bobbie K. Thurman, this stylish wearable celebrates the beauty of Pueblo Indian art.

Carver and teacher Bobbie K. Thurman proves his respect for the Native Americans of the Great Southwest every time he picks up a carving knife. That's because he specializes in kachina-style dolls. What are they? According to Bobbie, kachinas are the spiritual symbols used in ceremonies by the Hopi and other Pueblo peoples.

"There are probably 600 different kachina patterns," he explains. "They represent spirits involved in harvest, weather, hunting, birth, death—all aspects of life."

We liked Bobbie's colorful work so much that we asked him to provide a design for *WOOD*® magazine readers. Bobbie calls this pendant *Shalako,* a design based on the kachina that portrays a role in the rain ceremony.

Begin with basswood

For the pendant, you'll need a blank of basswood (or other fine-grained wood) measuring ½x2¾x5". Trace the pendant outline from the pattern. Then, mark a vertical centerline and reference lines for the front and back of the head, the bottom of the cape, and the skirt.

With a ½" No. 3 straight gouge, remove wood on the front and back of the headdress (leave the head full thickness for now) until it is about ⅛" thick. Next, slightly round the face mask and the back of the head.

Now, mark the necklace, collar, and front of the cape and carve them in. A ⅛" V-tool will work for detailing necklace lines.

After shaping the cape and folds with a ¼" No. 9 gouge, move to the legs and feet. Round the legs and boots. Use a ⅛" V-tool to define the soles and wrappings.

Feather the skirt

The shalako's skirt has seven rows of feathers, with each full row containing 12 feathers (front and back). The first row begins behind the necklace. Pencil in the first six rows evenly from top to bottom. Make the feathers in the seventh, or bottom, row a bit longer so that the other rows will appear to overlap.

Next, with a knife, make straight cuts into the wood (stop cuts) to define the feather rows. Then slice into the stop cut of each row at a slight angle to remove the chips that create the undercuts of the overlapping feathers. Now, define the feathers with a knife. Cut a center barb in each.

Paint on a colorful costume

After sanding your carving, smooth the surface by burnishing (rubbing) with the back of a gouge or a spoon. Then, seal the wood with satin-finish lacquer.

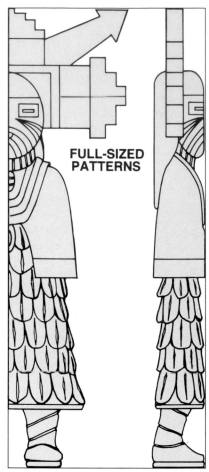

FULL-SIZED PATTERNS

You'll need acrylic paints in red, turquoise, black, white, burnt umber, and gold. Leave the cape and boots unpainted; the wood simulates deerskin.

When the paint has dried, rub on paste wax and buff. Add a screw eye to the top of the headdress and fit it with a lace.

Project Tool List
Gouges
  ½" No. 3
  ¼" No. 9
V-Tool, ⅛"
Carving knife

Note: Additional tools and equipment may be necessary to prepare a blank for the carving. Other styles and sizes of carving tools can be used in conjunction with or substituted for listed items.

THE HOWLIN' COYOTE

In the New Mexico wilds, you can count on coyotes howling. That's why carver Max Alvarez has a passion for this rascal of the sage. "They're survivors, and intelligent," he says.

Roughing out the body

Max carves large coyotes in cottonwood, but you can choose any carving wood. To make one the size Max usually carves, enlarge the pattern. For a smaller version, use the pattern on this page full-sized. (See the box at *right* for wood sizes.)

After transferring the pattern to your wood, saw out the body and tail. Cut a mortise in the body (the dimensions according to the size of your coyote) where the tail will go. Then, rough out the body, retaining its angles.

Next, rough out the tail. Saw a tenon at its base to fit the body's mortise. Next, finish-carve the tail and sand, but don't glue in place.

Getting down to the details

"Cut deep grooves to separate the toes on the coyote's feet," says Max. "And, make shallow squiggles for eyes." On each ear, hollow out an elongated trough. For the nostrils, drill two holes about ⅛" deep with a 1⁄16" bit. Use a ½" bit to drill a hole ¼" deep for the mouth. "Then, elongate the holes," he adds.

With the details carved, you're ready to sand, but not too smooth. "To leave some texture, I never use finer than 60-grit paper," he says. After sanding the body, glue the tail in place.

Pick your color, then paint

First, paint on a base coat of white (we recommend acrylic paints). When that dries, apply your chosen overall color, leaving the chest and underside white. After the second coat dries, apply black paint to the nose, mouth, eyes, ear accents, and tail tip. "Highlight the coat with streaks of black, then red, yellow, or other colors you like with a dry brush," Max notes.

Project Tool List
Bandsaw
Portable drill
Gouges or power-carving equipment
Carving knife

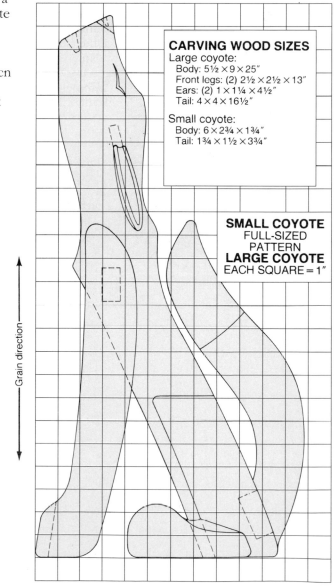

FRONT VIEW

BACK VIEW

Grain direction

CARVING WOOD SIZES
Large coyote:
 Body: 5½ × 9 × 25"
 Front legs: (2) 2½ × 2½ × 13"
 Ears: (2) 1 × 1¼ × 4½"
 Tail: 4 × 4 × 16½"

Small coyote:
 Body: 6 × 2¾ × 1¾"
 Tail: 1¾ × 1½ × 3¾"

SMALL COYOTE
FULL-SIZED PATTERN
LARGE COYOTE
EACH SQUARE = 1"

ROSCOE THE RACCOON

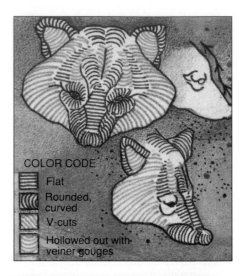

COLOR CODE
- Flat
- Rounded, curved
- V-cuts
- Hollowed out with veiner gouges

you through the detailing process as if you were enrolled in one of Desiree's carving classes. And, with a 70-percent complete, precarved rough-out, even novices will be successful.

Step 1: Roscoe the raccoon shapes up

Trace the full-sized pattern onto a 2½x3¾x5" piece of basswood or jelutong. Then, bandsaw the block to shape.

Begin carving by removing the excess wood until your rough has the curves and contours shown in the full-body views, right. "Be sure to leave about ½" of excess wood round the face," Desiree advises, "so you'll have plenty of area to work in all the angles and planes with small gouges and a knife."

Step 2: Carving a face for Roscoe

"The face is critical," Desiree says. "From the side, the muzzle is a triangle; the nose, an upside-down heart with the point removed."

To make it as easy as possible for you to carve your own Roscoe the Raccoon, blue-ribbon carver Desiree Hajny helped us develop these special, step-by-step instructions. The drawings, photos, and painting guide lead

Roscoe's unpainted face shows carved-in detail to imitate.

From the nose to a stop cut between the eyes, carve a flat, narrow bridge. Then, widen it up to the forehead. For an eye, cut a V-shape at the bridge for the upper lid and tear duct. Under it, make an inverted V-cut to start the lower lid. Outline the eye with curving stop cuts, then round the eyeballs. Fan the mask out for the ruffs of fur that extend behind and below the ears. For contour, see drawings *above*.

Step 3: Give your raccoon a fur coat

For the deep, narrow cuts that represent the heavier fur on the raccoon's rump, tail, legs, and ruffs, Desiree uses a ⅛"-wide parting tool

(V-tool), as shown in the photo at *left*. For the finer body hair that completely covers the back, thighs, head, face, and feet, she relies on an electric woodburning tool with interchangcable tips. You can simulate hair by stippling paint—short strokes applied with a No. 1 or smaller fine-tipped brush (see photo, *page 62*). Sand your carving smooth before burning-in the fur. If you paint the fur on, first seal the wood with tung oil or spray lacquer so the paint won't soak in.

Regarding woodburning, Desiree says, "Make small marks in layers, (as shown in the drawing, *page 63*). Use a fluid motion, and avoid putting in too many straight lines. Remember, gravity bends hair to a slight arc." Hair flows around an animal's body in tracts, following its contours. To see the direction of

continued

A V-tool carves the lines that represent heavy fur.

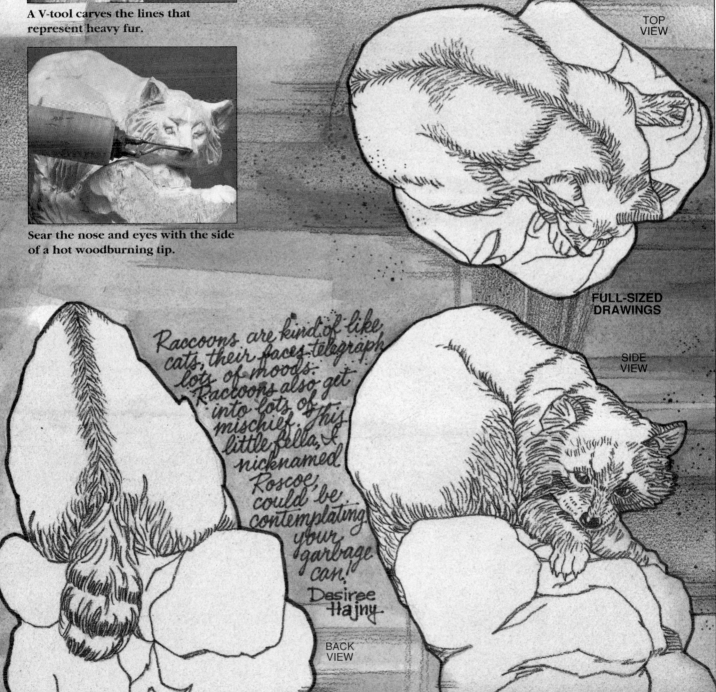

Sear the nose and eyes with the side of a hot woodburning tip.

TOP VIEW

FULL-SIZED DRAWINGS

SIDE VIEW

Raccoons are kind of like cats, their faces telegraph lots of moods. Raccoons also get into lots of mischief. This little fella, I nicknamed Roscoe, could be contemplating your garbage can!

Desiree Hajny.

BACK VIEW

61

CARVE ROSCOE THE RACCOON
continued

these tracts on a raccoon, study the detailed drawings, *right.* Use them as reference for your burned-in or painted-on hair marks.

To obtain shiny eyes and a nose on your carving, here's a tip from Desiree's workshop. "Sear the wood of the eyes and nose with the side of a hot wood-burning tip," she says. "This seals the wood as it darkens it. When you put on the coat of tung oil after painting, the seared areas won't absorb it, and they'll glisten." (Varnish over flat paint works, too.) Her technique, shown on *page 61,* works so well that at carving competitions, other carvers have accused Desiree of putting glass eyes in her animals!

Step 4: Paint brings Roscoe to life

After completing all burning, you're ready to begin Roscoe's paint job. Desiree paints only with acrylics, but oil will work just as well. "Whatever type of paint you choose, though," advises Desiree, "keep it thinned so the

Basic hair (fur) tracts of a raccoon

FRONT FACE

RIGHT BACK LEG

GENERAL BODY AREA

TAIL

RIGHT FRONT LEG

You can paint hair on with short brush strokes.

pigment doesn't clog up burn marks or carving details. To build color, use several thin coats rather than one thick one. You want to let

some of the natural wood color show through."

Desiree suggests that you follow this painting procedure: Apply light

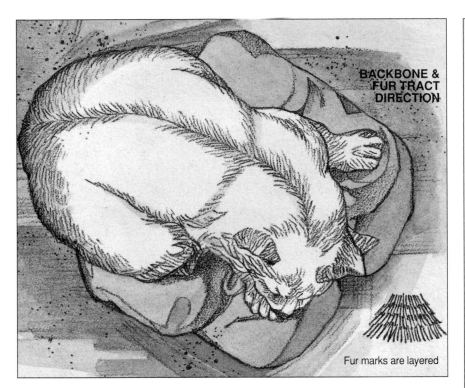

BACKBONE & FUR TRACT DIRECTION

Fur marks are layered

Supplies
Wood: 2½x3¾x5" basswood or jelutong (or precarved rough-out available from Ozark Mountain Crafts, Box R, Branson, MO 65616, or call 417-561-8275). For carving Roscoe, Desiree used the gouge and V-tool sizes and shapes as listed below. Gouges (general wood removal, shaping): ½" No. 3, ½" No. 5, ⅛" No. 7, ⅛", ¼" No. 9; Parting, or V-tools: (deep grooves and heavy fur) 45° in ¼", ⅛"; Knife: Bench style carving knife (general wood removal, stop cuts, fine lines, hair); Woodburner (for fur); Woodburning tips: spade, needle; Paint (acrylic or oil): white, black, brown, tan, gray; Clear finish: Tung oil; Brushes: Sable or camel hair, sizes 00, 0, 1, 3 (Paint and brushes available from art or hobby supply stores).

colors, then dark ones. That means that you'll want to paint all white areas first. Next, paint the brown-gray areas. Then, add black. Refer to the color keys to guide you as you paint.

After the paint has completely dried, you can begin the dry-brushing of the brown-gray areas with white mixed with tan. This adds realism to the fur. And, if you have never tried dry-brushing before; think of it as "painting with the bristles." That is, keep the paint and your brush dry enough that it doesn't flow onto your carving in a coat. Instead, the bristles of your brush leave behind only hints of color. Practice on paper first.

For the rock base Roscoe perches on, mix the colors you have used already. Create various shades by applying the paint in thin coats and adding darker colors in the crevices. After your painted carving dries, add a coat of tung oil.

Paint Colors

Eyes and nose—black, white underlining eyeballs.

Mask and outside of ears—black mixed with a touch of brown.

Bridge of muzzle upward to forehead—brown to black to tan.

Spots on muzzle—black or brown.

Muzzle, area above eyes, and inside of ears—white mixed with just a touch of tan or brown.

Body—brown mixed with gray, dry-brushed on top with an off-white for accent.

Front paws—dark brown/gray with black claws.

Back paws—light gray to dark gray with black claws.

Tail—brown/gray with three black stripes and black tip.

Boulders and rocks—gray/black to light gray, darker accents in crevices (mix up leftover raccoon body colors). Suggest moss or vegetation with dabs of green.

HERE'S OTTO THE OTTER

We asked Desiree Hajny to design another lifelike animal carving for you. Well, gather your gouges, gang; it's time to meet Otto the Otter.

Few creatures appear to enjoy life as much as otters. Invariably, they're shown sliding down slippery slopes, lolling about in the water, or just generally romping.

With this zesty personality in mind, champion wildlife carver Desiree Hajny perched Otto on a river rock, alert and itching to jump in. You almost can see Otto's tail switching as he surveys his stretch of river.

Get Otto into shape first

Trace the full-sized front- and side-view patterns onto your carving block, and bandsaw to shape.

Before you start carving, study Otto's build, the shape of his head, and his facial contours in the photos and illustrations. Then, begin carving with your knife and small gouges.

Turn your carving frequently as you work. Don't concentrate too much attention on any one area at this stage. Instead, remove wood from the entire carving to get the proper overall shape and proportion. And allow yourself

some room for detailing the head and face. About ½" of extra wood there should do the trick.

Continue your Otto-body work

Strive for a flowing surface as you carve Otto's body. Otters are sleek animals, so don't make yours too cylindrical or chunky.

If you were to cut a section across Otto's middle, you would have a triangle with bowed-out sides and base. His backbone ridge (most prominent between the shoulders and hindquarters) represents the tip of the triangle; his belly, the base.

The ridge disappears at the hips, Otto's widest point. Moving up front, study the photograph *left* before carving the shoulders and chest. Notice how the muscles appear like another layer, molded to the body.

Give Otto solid footing

Otters live around water and eat fish. To get about on soggy land, propel themselves through water, and snag food from the river, they have webbed, clawed feet.

Carve each foot to approximate shape; then, divide each into five toes with V-cuts (see illustration, *page 67*). Don't separate them completely—the feet won't look webbed if the cuts are too deep or too wide. Pick out the claws with your knife tip.

Put a good head on his shoulders

As the body takes shape, begin removing the excess wood from the head. Make the head about as thick as the neck from the side view, a little wider than the neck when viewed directly from the front. Otto's backbone line flows

END VIEW (REAR)

Frontal face contours

Hollowed contour

Rounded contour

Profile face contours

FRONT VIEW

The top of Otto's head shows a slight depression. His ears sit low on the sides of his head. Note the nose shape.

smoothly up his neck to the top of his head, where it changes to a slight depression (*above*).

From the side, Otto's head shows two major forms: a rough circle encompassing the ears, eyes, and jawline, and a blunt, half-egg shape for the muzzle. Viewed from the top, the head features appear slightly squared.

Shape the head with small gouges and a knife. The scooplike ears sit low, near the back of the head. Carve slight hollow spots in front of the ears, on the muzzle at the inside of the eyes, on top of the head, and under the nose.

With your knife, carve the nose as a baseball diamond shape with rounded upper sides. Place the eyes about midway along lines extending from the tip of the nose to the ear on each side, about the point where the egg-shaped muzzle joins the rounded head.

To carve the eyes, cut a gentle arc shape pointing upward with a downward-pointing one beneath it. Then, outline the eye with a series of curved stop cuts and carefully round the eyeball.

Complete carving the riverbed rock for Otto's perch. Then, sand or burnish Otto's head and
continued

CARVE OTTO THE OTTER
continued

body to smooth the contours and remove tool marks.

To burnish, rub the surface with a blunt object to compress the wood fibers. Some carvers do this with a small piece of wood while others use metal. An old teaspoon makes a good burnishing tool. With this done, you're ready to paint or woodburn the fine texture of Otto's fur.

First, study the illustration *opposite*. Notice how the hair grows, and the way it follows the contours of Otto's body.

Don't forget his fur coat

If you paint Otto's coat, seal the bare wood with tung oil or spray lacquer before you start. This prevents the paint from soaking in.

Paint the fur with a fine-tipped brush, size No. 1 or smaller.

Otto looks more realistic with his fur texture woodburned, and then painted. With a fine detail point on your woodburner, burn short, curving strokes in layers.

For shiny nose and eyes, sear them with the side of a hot wood-burning tip. The seared wood won't absorb tung oil (applied later), and will look shiny. You also could paint the nose and eyes with flat black paint, and then apply gloss varnish, clear fingernail polish, or clear epoxy over them.

Give Otto some color

Study the color photos and refer to the Finishing Materials and Paint

Colors listings, *opposite,* before you begin painting your carving.

Thin your paint. Make it watery, almost a wash, so the pigment doesn't fill in the woodburning marks or carved details.

Start with light colors and work toward darker shades, blending color changes to avoid harsh lines or a zebra effect. To build color, put on several thin coats.

Allow the paint to dry, and then dry-brush Otto with a mixture of white and brown paint. As the technique's name suggests, you start with a dry brush. You'll get better results if your paint is a little thicker, too.

Dip the brush into the paint lightly. Better yet, pat the paint surface with the brush just enough to pick up a

TOP VIEW

BACK VIEW

hint of color on the bristles. Then, brush your carving with light, quick strokes. Your best strokes will be the ones where you darn near miss Otto altogether with the brush.

You're not trying to put another layer of paint on Otto when you're dry-brushing. Rather, aim to put on the slightest amount of color as a frosty-looking highlight.

Mix some shades of gray for Otto's rock, and paint the base with browns and golds to represent a streambed. Dry-brush the rock and streambed with a light gray.

Inspect your work, and then sign and date it on the bottom. Finally,

coat your carving with low-gloss tung oil.

Paint Colors

Spots on muzzle, nose, eyes: black; Feet: brown-black (add black to dark brown); Belly, chin, chest, lower muzzle, neck: buff (add white to brown or parchment); Ears—brown; Back, top of head, nose, tail: varied brown shades; Rocks: varied grays; Base: gold, varied browns.

Supplies

Carving stock: Basswood, jelutong, or other carving wood. Tools:

Knife: bench carving knife; Gouges: ½" No. 3, ½" No. 5, ⅛" No. 7, ⅛" No. 9, ¼" No. 9; V-tool: ¼" 45°; Woodburner: fine detail tip; Finishing materials: acrylic artist's colors in parchment, dull white, bright white, black, dark brown, and gold; sable or camel-hair brushes, sizes 00, 0, 1, and 3; low-gloss tung oil.

Buying Guide

• **Precarved basswood roughout.** For current prices, contact Rossiter Ruff-outs and Carving Supplies, 1447 S. Santa Fe, Wichita, KS 67211, or call 800-8-BLANKS.

END VIEW

CHEST

Right hind foot is webbed

Five toes on each foot

Blend fur from brown to black

Right hind foot

NATURE'S-GOODNESS WALL PLAQUE

Red marks show the highest points in the still life. They are as high as the rim.

Now that he's retired, Robert Thomas, Jr., of Columbia, Maryland, spends most of his time carving wood. After 40 years as a graphic designer, he seems to have found a second career in carving.

His background in the graphic arts and appreciation of wood carving go together well, as evidenced by this strong, clean design on four relief levels. The harvest still life and the words from *The Lord's Prayer* combine to make a handsome decoration for kitchen or dining room. You'll get to try a cornucopia of techniques as you carve it, too.

Thomas loves carving, but he confesses that there is one aspect of it he finds pretty tough—coming up with ideas. We think he's come up with a great one here.

Getting down to work

Enlarge the pattern at *right* onto an 11X17" sheet with an enlarging photocopier. If starting with a roughout, go to "Digging into details" on *page 69.*

DEPTH GAUGE

GREEN = ⅛"
ORANGE = ¼"
GOLD = ⅜"
BROWN = ½"
TAN = Original height of blank

For a full-sized pattern, photocopy this illustration at 141 percent. Then copy that enlargement at 141 percent again to an 11X17" sheet.

Lay out the pattern on the bark side of your blank—the side that was toward the outside of the tree. (Check the end grain where the annual growth rings form arcs. The tops of those arcs point to the bark side).

Trace the pattern lines with a colored pencil so you can see where you've been. Use a straight-edge and French curve to maintain straight lines and smooth curves as you trace.

Remove the paper pattern, and straighten and redraw the lines as needed. Now, locate and mark the relief's high points as indicated on the pattern. After transferring the pattern, spray a light coat of artist's fixative or clear shellac over the plaque's surface to prevent smearing the lines.

Bandsaw the blank slightly outside the outermost pattern line, then sand down to the line. Rout the ¼" rabbet ⅜" deep around the plaque's edge. A ⁵⁄₁₆" piloted rabbet bit will do the trick.

Bringing the still to life

Make stopcuts around the still-life elements using a chip-carving knife or V-tool. (We chose a ¼" No. 41 V-tool.) Be sure to keep the side of the V-tool that is against the working edge vertical so you won't undercut the line or leave a sloping edge (see the photograph *above right*).

With the first round of stop-cutting done, move to the deepest relief area as shown on the pattern and begin *grounding* the plaque. This is the process of removing wood to establish the relief levels.

Copy the relief depth gauge, found next to the plaque pattern to light cardboard, such as an index card. Check the depths as you carve your way down to the final relief levels (see photo *right*). Don't try to get down to the final depth in one cut; take it in stages of stop-cutting and cleaning out. And, don't focus too closely on a particular area; move around the plaque, working each section a little at a time.

There isn't any one prescribed tool for grounding; the knife, gouges, and V-tools all will come

Hold the V-tool with the working edge vertical for stop cutting. Additional wood has been removed for clarity.

into play. A foam pad under the carving (we used carpet pad) is more convenient than a bench hook for holding this project.

Digging into details

When the grounding is done, start modeling the details. Redraw the wheat heads, the corn kernels, and the sun's face and rays. Trace another sun face onto scrap wood for a practice carving.

Study the face details in the photo on *page 70, top right* and the contours indicated by shading on the pattern as you fashion the face. Carve the mouth about ¹⁄₁₆" wide with your ¼" V-tool. Stop-cut around the smile lines, cheeks, nose, and eyes. Form the features with your ⅛" gouge and knife. Follow the shading to carve the contour under the nose and at the *continued*

Check relief levels during grounding with the depth gauge and a straight-edge. The color-coded pattern shows depths for grounding the plaque.

NATURE'S-GOODNESS WALL PLAQUE

continued

corners of the eyes. The deepest points are about ¹⁄₁₆". Check often for symmetry as you carve the face.

Try another technique

Now, you can turn to some chip-carving methods to detail the sun's rays. Begin with a stop-cut along the pattern line. Then, make angled, slicing cuts (photo *below right*) on each side of it to form a V about ⅛" deep and ³⁄₁₆" wide at each ray.

Do the same for the lines on the wheat heads, but make your Vs narrower-about ¹⁄₁₆". Square up the line separating the wheat heads and cut it to about ³⁄₁₆" wide with straight, vertical sides.

Carving the corn

Start from the high point on the left husk and taper down to about ⅛" below the surface at the top of the loaf. Develop a pleasing curve and round over the edges as you carve. Make a stopcut along the line between the husks and carve the right husk about ¹⁄₁₆" lower than the left. Separate the kernels with chip-carved lines.

Making the bread

The bread loaf is carved in perspective, so you'll be carving down from the high point in two directions. Study the detail photograph and the pattern shading as you taper the loaf to about ¼" below the surface at its right end. Depths to the left of the high point vary. Carve the top corner of the loaf to be slightly higher than the sun's face—¹⁄₁₆" is fine—and work down to about ¼" deep where the loaf meets the orange.

Stop-cut the line separating the top and bottom of the loaf with the V-tool, keeping the vertical side of the tool toward the top of the loaf. Follow the shading on the pattern to complete the loaf and finish the two fruit shapes.

A close up of the still life shows the relationship of the major elements. Shallow cuts create the details of the sun's face.

Meet the lettering challenge

Now, it's time to try out your lettering skills. Clean cuts, straight lines, and vertical sides are crucial, particularly in the low-relief, monument-style lettering you'll be doing here. Take your time and keep your tools honed for sharp-looking lettering.

Stop-cut the letters with the ⅛" V-tool as shown *opposite, top*. Make stopcuts on the inside curves of letters (such as the inside of the O) with a ⅛" No.7 gouge. Stab the gouge vertically into the work surface and rotate it slightly to carve the inside radius (see photo *opposite, bottom left)*. Connect the radius cuts with straight knife cuts and pop the interior waste out. After the lettering is completed, use

Make slicing cuts with the chip knife when detailing the sun's rays. Carve the corn kernels and wheat heads the same way.

Stop-cut the letters with your ⅛"
V-tool. Keep the cutting edge
vertical so that the sides of the
letters will be straight.

With a No. 7 gouge held vertically,
make a twisting cut to stop cut the
curved interior lines on the letters.

the shallow gouge to pare the faces
of the letters down about ⅛" below
the rim of the plaque.

Wrapping things up

When you're finished, take a
close look at your carving—a final,
critical inspection. Touch up any
cuts that aren't quite right and clean
out fuzzy spots. Sand the uncarved,
raised rim to remove traces of
fixative, but don't sand the carved
areas. They don't need it, and,
anyway, you don't want to remove
any of your tool marks—they're
part of the character and texture of
hand-carved work.

We used watercolors to finish the
lettering and still life, but thinned
artist's acrylic colors work great,
too. You can follow the scheme
shown in the color photograph on
page 68 or devise your own. We
gave the deepest relief area two
applications of Watco medium
walnut stain and put a single
application on the area behind
the lettering. Finally, we applied
Watco oil finish to the entire
plaque before hanging it up for
all to enjoy.

Supplies

You'll need a 2x9x17" slab
for your carving. We used
butternut, a hardwood that
carves easily and finishes
beautifully. You also could
choose basswood, jelutong,
or sugar pine.

Or, order a presawed blank
or a 70-percent roughout in
either butternut or basswood.
For current prices, contact
Rossiter's Ruff-outs and
Carving Supplies, 1447 S.
Santa Fe, Wichita, KS 67211,
or call 800-8-BLANKS.

Knives: Chip carving knife,
Bench knife

Gouges: ¼" No. 3, ¾" No. 3, ⅛"
No. 7, ¼" No. 7,

⅛" No. 41 V-tool, ¼" No. 41
V-tool

Strop and slipstone

Finishing materials: Watercolors or acrylic paints in
green, red, orange, yellow,
and magenta; Walnut oil
stain; Clear finishing oil.

TABLETOP CIGAR-STORE INDIAN

In the days before public education was guaranteed, many people couldn't read and write. So, to sell their goods and services, merchants and professionals put carved displays and symbolic signs outside their shops and offices to denote what they offered. An optometrist, for example, might hang a large pair of carved eyeglasses; a cobbler a boot; a tavern keeper a tankard; a dentist a tooth, and so on.

But none of these "shop figures," as collectors call them, has become more recognizable and sought after than the tobacco- or cigar-store Indian. And the account of how the Indian became such a well-known symbol is an interesting tale.

It's said that Sir Walter Raleigh introduced tobacco grown and smoked by the Indians in the Virginia Colony to England in the early 1600s. The popular product became known as "Indian weed" and storekeepers specialized in its sale. However, to promote tobacco cleverly posed a problem—at least until a pioneer advertising genius thought to associate an Indian figure with the puffable leaf.

As the story goes, few people in England at the time knew what a New-World Indian actually looked like. News from Virginia, though, did tell them that some of the colonists employed black slaves to tend the crops. So, it's said that the first tobacco-store Indian was a black man wearing a feathered headdress and a kilt of tobacco leaves!

It took about 100 years for the carved figure we recognize as a cigar-store Indian to appear in the American colonies. But from 1840 to 1900 (when they began to be replaced by metal signs) the cigar-

store Indian was everywhere. It has been estimated that at the turn of the century there were 100,000 of them in use. Fifty years later, the number had dropped to 3,000, and today wooden cigar-store Indians are rare.

Traditional cigar-store Indian figures were most often life-sized. The one on these pages, however, measures just 19½" tall—a size adaptable to many display possibilities.

Carver Mike Krone of Branson, Missouri, designed this version. In addition to size, he deviated from the traditional by "westernizing" the clothes and headdress to depict clothing worn by the Plains Indians. "This tends to create a more striking carving," notes Mike, who formerly carved nothing but western figures. He now focuses on carvings of animals and sports figures as an associate of Mountain Woodcarvers, a noted Branson woodcarving shop.

Define your carving

If you have ordered the roughed-out carving, skip down to the next paragraph. If you're starting from scratch, first enlarge the front and side view patterns given on *page 75* to full-size, then trace them on your carving block. Next, bandsaw the block to shape.

Because of the figure's size, it's easy to hold for carving with palm-sized tools by bracing against your thigh. But, the rectangular base also lends itself to clamping in place should you have larger carving tools.

With your knife or a gouge, begin at the base and take off excess wood until you achieve the Indian's rough shape. On a pre-carved roughout, start surfacing (removing the machining marks) with a knife or gouge. Work on the legs, torso (leave the hands alone for the time being), and arms first, then move to the base.

There, as shown *below,* use your gouge to do the surfacing, and carve deeply enough to shape the feet and give them thickness (about ½" will do).

Now, following the principle that you should work from less-detailed areas to more-detailed areas in order to familiarize yourself with the tools and the wood, work from the feet up to the figure's neck. Carve wood away to define (outline) parts such as the moccasins, the legs, the arms (not hands), braids, and neck with stop cuts from your knife and slices from the gouge.

When you complete defining, go back and carve in details such as fringe and hair with your V-tool. (Novice carvers should save carving the fringe detail around the hand areas until the hands have been shaped.)

Begin surfacing your figure at the base with a No. 3 gouge. Outline the moccasined feet, then define them.

Shape the hands from mittens

To carve the left hand with your knife or gouge, don't launch into the fingers right away. Instead, consider the hand's general shape and where the fingers and thumb originate by studying your own hand. You'll notice that the thumb begins down on the side of the hand, as shown in the photo *above right,* but not exactly where the fingers do.

Here's an easy way to carve the hand: First draw a mitten on the

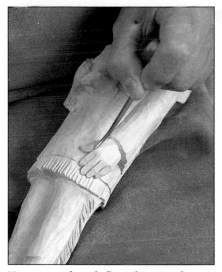

To carve a hand, first draw and shape a mitten, then divide the mitten into fingers with cuts of your V-tool.

wood, then carve it. Next, take your pencil and divide the finger portion of the mitten into separate fingers, noting the different length of each. With your V-tool, carve the fingers, as shown in the photo *above.*

Now, start on the right hand, remembering that it, too, should begin as a mitten, but one that surrounds and supports the cigars, as shown below. After you have carved the fingers, use your V-tool to make the cigars appear bundled by a ribbon. A simple crosshatch pattern outlines the top of the cigar bundle.

The right hand holds and supports the cigars. Define individual cigars and the band around them with a V-tool.

The challenge of the head and headdress

Carving the face will be the most critical aspect of your cigar-store Indian. To get a realistic one, you must adhere to the facial characteristics shown in the closeup photo of the painted figure on *page 74.* Carve the cheekbones set wide apart. And make the lips full and rounded, but not overly prominent.

To start the face, pencil it on the wood, as in the photo, *below.* First, draw a broad oval divided by a vertical center line (this helps you keep the face symmetrical). Next, draw the eyes, noting that they should be widely spaced (about one eye-width apart) and about two-thirds of the way up the face.

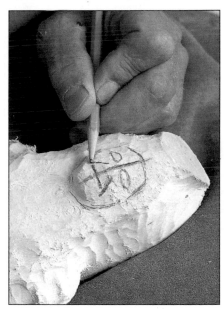

Draw a large oval on the wood for the face, then divide it with a vertical line to help you keep features in balance. Redraw the lines as necessary.

Draw the smile lines of the mouth with two lines forming the legs of the letter A. Begin the lines at the nostrils and run them downward and outward to nearly intersect with the horizontal line of the mouth that falls between the tip of the chin and the tip of the nose. Remember that on the average human face, the width of the mouth equals the distance between the pupils of the eyes.

continued

TABLETOP CIGAR-STORE INDIAN
continued

Now, use your knife and gouges to shape facial features, as in the photo *below*. As you carve, lightly redraw the vanishing pencil lines.

Refer to the closeup photo of the painted head and the rear view to carve and detail the headdress. Note that the feathers taper out from the head to a thickness of about ³⁄₁₆". Define the feather outlines, and the quill and barb of each feather, with your V-tool. (See how the feathers appear in the photo of the finished face.)

Study the facial features closely. Note that the smile lines come down from the nose like the legs of the letter A.

Complete your carving at the base

Return now to the base of the figure and touch up any rough surfaces you might have missed. Then, draw to size on a piece of paper the logo shown on the base in the opening photograph. With carbon paper, transfer your logo to the front of the base. Carve it with your V-tool (woodburning the design on the base also would be a nice touch).

To complete the carving, use your gouge or knife to add a few wrinkles to the figure's clothing. Generally, wrinkles appear inside the elbows, on the lower front of the shirt, and at the knees, as you can see in the front view of the completed figure.

Now, add the color

For the Indian's buckskin breeches and shirt, thin the paint so that it acts as a stain and lets the grain show through. Use a similar thinned-down mixture on the face, also. For accent, the fringe should be colored with full-strength paint (or use a woodburner to darken it before painting). The headdress, braid trappings, and cigar wrapping all require solid, unthinned paint.

To give your cigar-store Indian an antique look, add a small amount of burnt umber artist's oil color (or walnut oil stain) to boiled linseed oil, then coat the figure. Be sure to first test your antiquing mixture on a piece of scrap wood.

Supplies

The cigar-store Indian requires a 4¾"x3¾"x19½" block of basswood or other carving wood. You can, though, get a quicker start by ordering the 70-percent complete, precarved roughout shown *left*.

For current prices, contact Ozark Mountain Crafts, Drawer R, Branson, MO 65616.

As a minimum, you'll need the carving tools illustrated below:

Knife:
Bench-type carving knife

Gouges:
½" No. 3 gouge;
⅛–³⁄₁₆" 45° V-tool

Finishing Materials: 80–120-grit sandpaper; Water-soluble, acrylic artist's paints in white, red, blue, orange, brown, and yellow; No. 7 or No. 8 brush, No. 000 brush; Boiled linseed oil; Burnt-umber artist's oil color (or walnut oil stain).

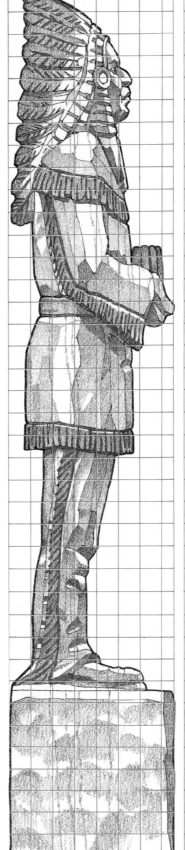

CIGAR STORE INDIAN

Each Square= ½"

THE NORWEGIAN BACHELOR FARMER

Flat-plane carving had its origins in the rustic and rugged peasant carvings done in Scandinavia 150–200 years ago, according to Harley J. Refsal, carver and instructor in Scandinavian folk art at Luther College, Decorah, Iowa. "The style takes its name from the flat planes created with the knife cuts, a technique that at first glance seems rough and unsophisticated. But, the knife marks that shape the piece become a part of it—when you take away wood with the blade or gouge, you create an element," he explains. "A cut to remove wood from the leg becomes a heavy crease in the pants. In flat-plane carving you don't shape the figure, then go around putting knife cuts in to smooth it."

Harley learned flat-plane carving in Norway in 1965, and has practiced the style ever since. In fact, in 1989 and 1990, he returned to the land of its origin to teach the technique to Norwegians—all the folk-art carvers had passed away.

The figures Harley carves represent the kinds of people he grew up with in rural Hoffman, Minnesota. And the flat-plane style suits them. "It's a rough-hewn way of depicting rough-hewn people," Harley says, "like this Norwegian bachelor farmer, made famous by

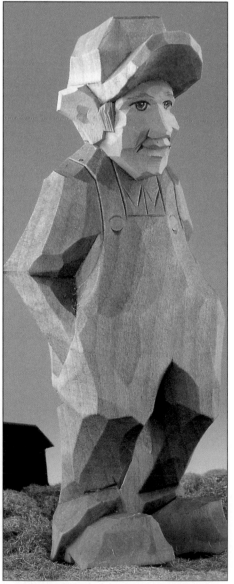

Garrison Keillor's book *Lake Wobegon Days*. But remember, a caricature isn't supposed to be realistic, so features that stick out, such as ears, feet, cap, etc., must be larger than life."

After assembling all the tools and supplies you'll need for this project (see list, *page 79),* study the front- and back-view photographs of the completed farmer. And, turn to the closeup photograph of the figure's

face on *page 79.* In the full-figure photos, note the sharp, prominent cuts that produce creases and folds, elbows and knees. Study the facial close-up to see how each angular cut of the knife defines a feature— nose, cheeks, ear. Now, you're ready to start carving.

Carve from the bottom up

With your knife, shape the figure's legs, as in photo *opposite, top left.* Be sure that you don't round the legs so they resemble perfect cylinders—the goal is to leave as many large, flat planes as possible. Take advantage of the cuts to make folds and creases. Imagine that if you sawed off one of the figure's legs midway between knee and ankle, and looked at the cross-section, the shape would be octagonal rather than round.

For the crotch of the farmer's pants, make two strongly defined cuts in an upside-down "V" shape. And, don't cut the crotch in too high. Locate it no more than ½" from the spot where his legs join the trunk of his body.

Now, turn the figure over and shape the seat of the farmer's overalls with your knife blade. In the photo *opposite, bottom left* you can see the bold V-cuts required to form a crease—one cut down and in, the next up and in to meet it.

Now that you have carved his seat, turn your attention and your blade to the feet. Note how large the shoes appear in the photos. There's a double reason for this. First, you must leave them large to

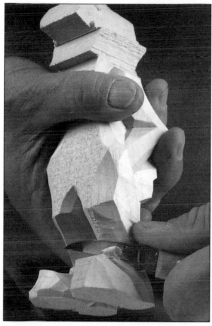

Bold knife strokes shape the leg. Remember, the cut you create stays there.

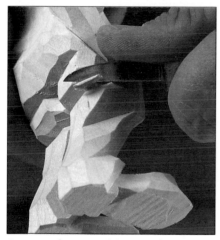

One cut down and in, another up and in make a fold in the cloth.

provide a solid base for the figure to stand on. Second, their size is part of the caricature.

Carve the shoes without attention to detail, avoiding the natural tendency to round them. Let a minimum number of flat cuts define their shapes. For the soles, for instance, you need only to trim the wood with flat, thin, vertical cuts around the edge of the shoe. Any attempt to accent the sole by making it a protrusion can result in a break-off of the cross grain (something to remember when you get to the cap

visor, too). Let the farmer's pant legs fall all the way to the ground in back (see rear-view photo), but make cuts to represent folds where his pants break on top of his shoes (see back-view photo at *right*).

Put his hands in his pockets

Before carving the farmer's arms, plan your cuts so his hands will disappear into his overall pockets. And, as with the legs, avoid carving perfect cylinders. Instead, try to make large, flat cuts that meet sharply at the edge of the wood, as if his shirt had been starched and ironed.

Separate the arms from the body at the chest with cuts to form a wide-legged "V" on the inside of the elbow (for detail, see photo on the *next page, top right*). These cuts also narrow and define the width of his chest.

The widest part of the figure is the area where the hands enter the pockets. And, the hands in those pockets tend to push out the overalls, so leave more wood at those points.

When you're satisfied with the look and shape of his arms, turn the farmer over to work on the back.

With a ½" No. 6 or No. 7 gouge, cut across the grain (horizontally) with scooping motions to remove wood between the arms. This creates the small of his back. (Here, the gouge makes it difficult to leave flat planes, but try to keep gouge marks to a minimum.) Leave each arm ½" wide at the outer elbow. Then, clean up the elbows with the same type of cuts you used on the inner elbows—sharp edges on the elbows are okay (see elbow, *above right* and *right*). After the elbows, you will have shaped your farmer from the neck down.

Character for a caricature

Before starting to carve the head, draw on large ears and sideburns as shown on the pattern and the photo *page 78, top left*. Don't be afraid to exaggerate. Place the ear at least two-thirds of the way back on the side of the head. Then, with your knife, remove wood from in front of, on top of, and behind the ear

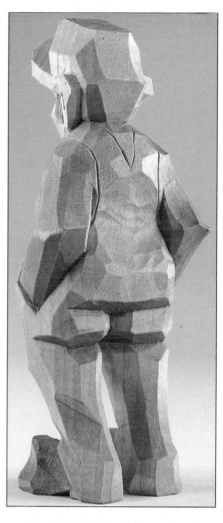

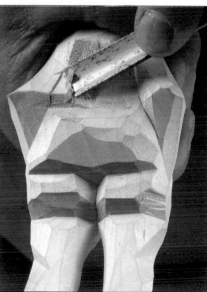

A gouge removes wood to form the small of the back.

continued

THE NORWEGIAN BACHELOR FARMER
continued

so that it protrudes about ¼" at the thickest point (just below and behind the top).

Next draw on the line for his seed cap. (Note that the cap goes all the way down to his collar behind the ears.) Then, narrow the wood of the cap over the face so the visor ends up sticking out about ½" from the side of the farmer's head, as shown in the photo *far right*.

By now, you have probably trimmed off the sideburn outlines, so draw them in again.

Note: *While working on the ears and sideburns, constantly check both sides of the head to see that the ears are level with each other and the same approximate size.*

Then, recess the area below and in front of the ears about ½2", as in the photo of the finished face, *opposite.*

Taper the front part of the ears so that they disappear under the sideburns. To detail the inside of the ear, make a stabbing cut with the point of a ⅛"–⅜6" No. 9 gouge, as in photo *above, far right*. Then, with the same tool, make a few shallow sweeps from the surrounding wood and into the cut.

Next, shape the underside of the cap visor with a shallow ¼"-⅜" No. 4 or 5 gouge. Run the tool carefully from front to back and toward the forehead. With your knife, remove wood from the top side of the visor to follow the curvature you carved on the underside. *Use caution at this stage.* You're carving across grain, and if you make the visor thinner than ⅜6", or exert too much pressure with a tool, it can break off. Make a stopcut on the forehead under the visor to help shape the face.

Now, you're ready to tackle the face—often thought of as the most difficult step in carving. So, proceed slowly and refer to the photo of the finished face, *opposite.*

Begin by drawing a vertical centerline down the front of the

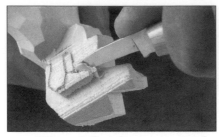

Pencil lines define the exaggerated ears and sideburns.

Detail ears with a simple stab cut from a small gouge.

face. Then, remove wood with your knife at an outwardly sloping angle toward the back of the head. (If you look at someone's face, it isn't flat, but tapers toward the tip of the nose.)

To form the smile lines on both sides of the nose, make V-cuts with your knife. Note that they begin at the bulb or fattest part of the nose, then run down and outward like the legs of the letter A. With a shallow V-cut, make the mouth, noting that it's located on the face slightly closer to the nose than to the tip of the chin. Accent the lower lip by cutting a shallower and shorter V-cut below and parallel to the mouth.

Using the same V-cuts as above, shape the eye sockets, at the same time thinning and forming the nose. With your small No. 9 gouge, scoop out the final sockets. You'll paint in the eyes later.

Now, it's time to add a few details. For the overall suspenders, first draw on lines, then vein (lightly cut) them with your V-tool.

Note the thick cap visor. If you carve it too thin, though, or use excess pressure, the cross-grained wood could break

Vein the eyebrows, sideburns, and shirt collar as well. To make the brass buttons on his overalls, use the same stab technique you did to detail the inner ear. And, before you put away your tools, take the V-tool and add your name and the date to the bottom of one of the carved figure's shoes.

Paint that shows the grain

Referring to the photos *here* and on *page 76*, paint your farmer. Remember to thin the paints with water so the grain will show through (except the colors you use for the eyes, which should be opaque). Experiment first.

Thinned acrylic paints allow the wood grain to show. Add a patina by slightly darkening linseed oil with stain.

After the paint on your carving has thoroughly dried, liberally apply boiled linseed oil to which you've added just a hint of brown oil-stain or burnt umber artist's oil color. This gives your figure a protective patina.

FULL-SIZED PATTERN

GRAIN DIRECTION

SIDE VIEW

FRONT VIEW

Supplies

The farmer requires a 2¼x2¼x6½" block of basswood on which to transfer the pattern shown at *left*. Or, start with the prime northern basswood blank sawn from two directions, shown *opposite, bottom right*. It has lines drawn to get you going. For current prices, contact Harley Refsal Wood-carving, 619 North St., Decorah, IA 52101. Also available: a book containing 20 patterns of Harley's favorite figures.

You'll need the carving tools illustrated *below*:

Knives: Bench-type carving knife

Gouges: ½" No. 6 or 7 palm gouge, ¼"–⅜" No. 4 or 5 gouge, ⅛"–³⁄₁₆" No. 9 gouge, ⅛" 45° V-tool

Finish Materials: Water soluble, acrylic artist's paints in white, red, blue, green, brown, and yellow (or any other color you care to substitute), No. 7 or No. 8 brush, No. 000 brush; Boiled linseed oil; Burnt-umber artist's oil (or brown oil stain).

CARVE A CANVASBACK

When Jim Barnett, a local carver, showed me his duck wall plaque, I was impressed, but skeptical. I have a hard time carving the Thanksgiving turkey, much less this eye-catcher. "Not to worry," Jim assured me. "All you need are just a few carving tools, one piece of ¾" stock, a child's watercolor set, and some step-by-step instructions." Sure enough, within two hours, I had my project all carved and ready for finishing. I was so pleased with the results, I decided to present the carving to my father, an avid hunter.

Cut the stock and transfer the pattern

1. Cut a piece of ¾"-thick stock to 5" wide by 14½" long. (We used butternut; see the Buying Guide for our source. You also could select walnut, sugar pine, basswood, chestnut, white pine, jelutong, or Ponderosa pine.)

2. Mark a reference line 1" from the bottom edge of the blank. With carbon paper, transfer the full-sized Duck pattern on *pages 82–83* to the carving blank, aligning the bottom of each duck's body with the marked reference line.

3. Rout or cut a 45° chamfer along the face edges of the blank.

4. Using the full-sized pattern for reference, mark an oval reference line around the duck-body outlines. You'll need the oval for cut locations when removing the background material later.

Let the carving begin

Note: Relief carvers employ a variety of setups to secure their workpieces. We prefer a bench hook like the one shown below. By placing your carving blank on the base, you can comfortably carve in several directions before turning the blank around. Secure the clamp board in the jaws of your vise to hold it steady. Always carve toward one of the support strips—never toward your body.

1. With a ³⁄₁₆" or ¼" V-parting tool, cut on the outside of the marked line to carve the outline of both ducks as shown in the photo

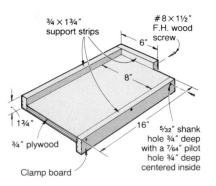

¾ × 1¾"
support strips

#8 × 1½"
F.H. wood
screw

6"

8"

1¾"

16"

¾" plywood

⁵⁄₃₂" shank
hole ¾" deep
with a ⁷⁄₆₄" pilot
hole ¾" deep
centered inside

Clamp board

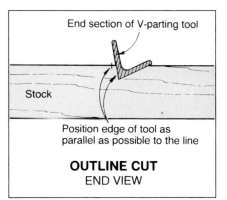

End section of V-parting tool

Stock

Position edge of tool as
parallel as possible to the line

OUTLINE CUT
END VIEW

opposite, top left. See the Buying Guide at the end of the article for our source of tools. See the drawing *above* for reference when angling your tool to make the cut. Do not carve away the line. If you're right-handed, drive the tool with your right hand and guide the tool with your left. Jim Barnett, the carver shown in the photos throughout this article, happens to be left-handed. (We made our first outlining cuts about ⅛" deep. Then, we carved a second and third set of cuts, deepening the groove to about ⅜".) The normal cutting depth for a low-relief carving is half the thickness of the wood.

2. With a ⅜" or ½" no. 7 gouge, remove the stock (a process called grounding) between the oval reference line and V-groove outline as shown in the photo *opposite bottom left*. To make these cuts,

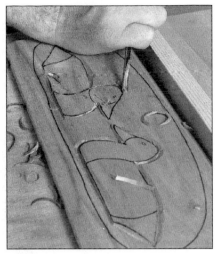

Cutting just outside the marked outline, use a V-parting tool to outline both the drake and hen bodies.

With a ⅜" or ½" gouge, start just inside the marked oval to remove the background next to the duck.

start just on the inside of the marked oval reference line, and with the scooping motion shown in the drawing titled Grounding the Background, push the gouge into the wood at about a 45° angle. Lay the tool nearly flat as you take out the long slices. Do not make the bottom of the grounding cut deeper than the V-grooved outline cuts.

3. Utilize the V-parting tool to remove splinters at the end of the gouge grounding cuts and next to the V-cuts where shown on the drawing *above right*.

GROUNDING THE BACKGROUND

After grounding, clean this area with the V-parting tool.

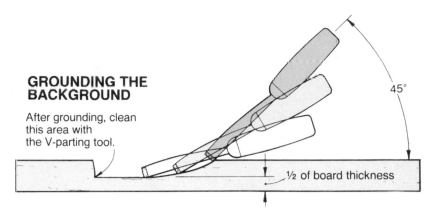

45°

½ of board thickness

4. With a ⅜" No. 3, 4, or 5 gouge, make shallow cuts to round over the edges of both duck bodies as shown in the photo *below*.

5. Using a V-parting tool, make a shallow V-cut for the lower mandible (a duck's lower bill) on each duck. See the full-sized Duck pattern on the *following pages* for reference. Utilizing the same tool, make a shallow cut for the nostril on each bill. Then, make an even shallower cut where the bill meets the head (this cut separates the head and bill, and simplifies painting the ducks later).

6. With a ⅜" No. 6 gouge, make a single pass to form the eye channel and cheek. Next, use the gouge to form the neck recess as shown in the photo *below right* and located on the full-sized pattern.

7. With the V-parting tool, make three cuts to form the wing feathers on the back of each duck body. Repeat the process to form the tail feathers.

8. Utilizing the ⅜" No. 5 gouge, smooth out the tool marks on each duck. Make very shallow cuts to remove the high spots.

Color brings the ducks to life

Note: We painted our ducks with a child's watercolor set and a ¼" brush. Lightly apply the paint to the wood to avoid hiding the grain. To darken an area, use several light coats instead of one heavy coat.

1. With a ¼" brush, paint the drake's breast and tail section black. Carefully paint the areas just next to the background to avoid

continued

Make shallow cuts with the gouge to round over the outside edges of both duck bodies.

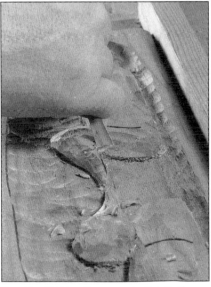

Use the ⅜" No. 6 gouge to form the neck recess. Start at the neck center and work to the outside.

CARVE A CANVASBACK
continued

having the paint bleed onto the background. If it does bleed, make a shallow cut with a gouge to remove the colored portion of the background.

2. Mix black and just a dab of yellow ochre to paint the bills. Mixing the yellow with the black results in a lighter, more natural-colored bills. Apply light coats. If the color is too transparent after it dries fully, add another coat.

3. Mix a light gray for the body portion of both ducks by blending white and just a touch of black. Brush on the paint.

4. Using burnt umber (medium brown), paint the head, breast, and tail area of the hen.

Paint the drake's eye red with a fine-tipped brush.

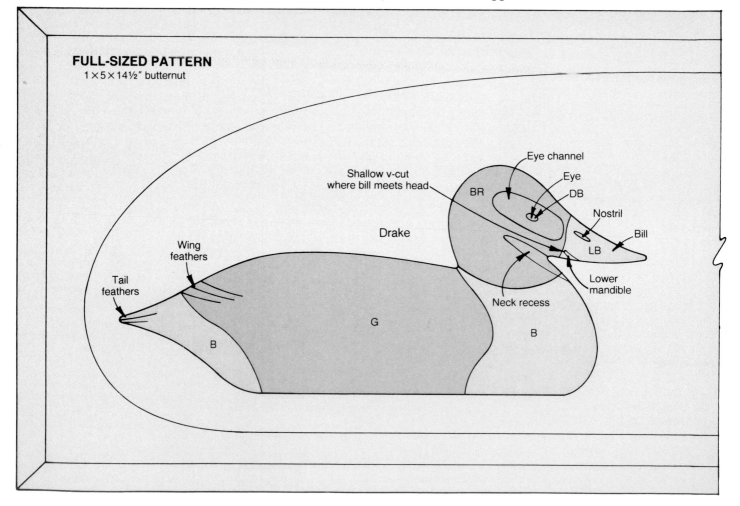

FULL-SIZED PATTERN
1 × 5 × 14½″ butternut

Eye channel

Shallow v-cut where bill meets head

Eye

BR

DB

Nostril

Bill

Drake

LB

Wing feathers

Lower mandible

Tail feathers

Neck recess

G

B

B

5. Mix red and burnt umber to form a brick-red color, and paint the drake's head.

6. Using a fine-tipped brush, paint the drake's eye red and the hen's eye dark brown. To avoid smudging or running, let the paint dry completely before painting the pupils in the next step.

7. With a black fine-tipped felt marker or the tip of a fine brush, add the black pupil to each duck's eye. To prevent smudging, let the paint dry for an hour or two before applying the sealer (if necessary, you can speed up the process with a hair dryer).

8. Lightly wipe on a finish. (We left the butternut natural and sealed the wood with Watco Danish Oil.) The oil slightly darkens the butternut, making the use of a stain unnecessary.

Supplies
¾×5×14" carving blank, water colors, clear satin finish (oils work well).

Buying Guide
• **Carving tools.** ¼" V-parting tool, Catalog No: 18A52; ⅜" No. 6 gouge, Catalog No. 18C11; ⅜" No. 5 gouge, Catalog No. 18A41. Complete kit of three tools, Catalog No. 18A61 (for the set). For current prices, contact Woodcraft, 210 Wood County Industrial Park, P.O. Box 1686, Parkersburg, WV 26102, or call 800-225-1153.
• **Butternut.** ¾×5×14½".
For current prices, contact The Woodcraft Shop, 2724 State Street, Bettendorf, IA 52722, or call 800-397-2278 or 319-359-9684.

Project Tool List
Gouges
⅜" No. 3, 4, or 5
⅜" No. 6
⅜" or ½" No. 7
V-Tools, 3/16", ¼"

COLOR KEY
B - black
LB - light black
G - gray
BU - burnt umber
BR - brick red
DB - dark brown

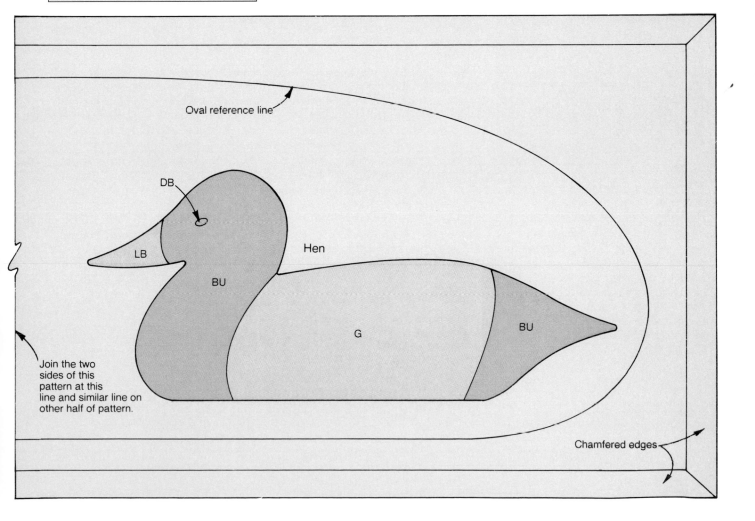

CARVE A CARDINAL

By day, Lindel Porter, directs the respiratory therapy program at Tulsa City College, but at day's end he heads for his workshop. There, he carves eagles, waterfowl, and songbirds. And, when he's not carving, he's watching. "I study the birds that come to the bird feeder. But, I enjoy the cardinals best. They light up our landscape."

Section your bird

"To resist breakage, I carve the cardinal's head, tail, and body separately," notes Lindel. Following the grain directions shown *opposite,* bandsaw the head, tail, and body from a 2x2x8" basswood block. "On the bandsaw, notch out the pointed feathers at the rear [see side view]. Leave them ¼" thick for detailing," he says.

Shape up the body first

With a knife, a No. 3 or 5 gouge, or a power-carving bit, round the body to the neck-joint. Next, outline the feather pattern with a knife or V-tool, undercutting each feather so that it stands out from the body, as in detail photo, *opposite.* Next, round the feathers off slightly so they conform to the body, then detail the quills and barbs.

Attend to the head

Round and shape the head. Then, define the bill's outline. "Use undercuts to slightly recess the lower bill and a tiny V-cut for the nostrils," says Lindel. Mark eye locations, and with a ⅜" bit drill sockets ⅛" deep.

Carve the area to be joined to the body so that the two pieces come together cleanly. "Make the bird more lifelike," suggests the craftsman, "by tilting the head." Then, glue the head to the body and let dry. For hidden joints, Lindel cuts a shallow, V-shaped trough on the glue lines, fills it with wood putty, then, after it dries, sands the joint to blend with the wood.

Mount 7mm glass eyes (see the Buying Guide) in the head by first filling the sockets with soft wood putty. Push the eyes about one-third their diameter into the putty, then shape the squeeze-out to form upper and lower eyelids. If you don't shape eyelids, the eyes will look too large.

Tarry on the tail

For realism, the tail must fan out and curve—like a sail filling with wind. "Hollow the underside of the tail," instructs the carver. "Then, trace the feather pattern, undercut and round them, and detail the quills and barbs."

Join the tail to the body by cutting a slot to match tail width and curvature in the underside of the rear body. Dry-fit the parts, then glue in place. "Strengthen the joint by drilling a ⅛" hole through the tail and into the body to fit a ⅛" dowel," says Lindel. "Dip the dowel in glue and then push it in place."

Wet-on-wet for natural color

"I use acrylics," says Lindel, "and first I paint on a base coat of three parts Gesso [a thickening medium] to one part burnt umber and one part mars black. I thin this wash to a milklike consistency." To duplicate Lindel's wet-on-wet painting technique, which allows details to show through, thin your colors or mix of colors to wash-consistency, then paint them on coat by coat until you've built up the color saturation you want. Refer to the color key *opposite top.*

Get the cardinal on its feet

To attach the pewter feet (see Buying Guide), drill ⅛" holes in the body where shown. Dip the feet-insertion wires in glue and insert in the holes. Paint after the glue dries, then mount by inserting the short pegs on the feet into holes drilled in a piece of branch. Add a base.

Buying Guide
•**Pewter feet, 7mm glass eyes**. For current prices, contact Little Mountain Carving Supply, Rt. 2, Box 1329, Front Royal, VA 22630. Free catalog. 800-752-7573 or 703-636-3125.

Project Tool List
Bandsaw
Portable drill
Carving knife
Gouges
   ⅜" No. 5
   ³⁄₁₆" and ⅜" No. 7
   ¼" No. 8
   ⅛" No. 9
V-Tools, ⅛", ¼"

COLOR KEY
1. Red shaded areas—cadmium red dark
2. Black areas—3 parts mars black to one-half part thalo blue
3. Beak—cadmium red light and cadmium yellow medium
4. Top of head—cadmium red light highlighted by cadmium yellow light
5. Back—one part cadmium red dark to ⅟₁₆ part thalo blue
6. Body and feather highlights—cadmium red light
7. Back and underside—cadmium red medium to cadmium red light to cadmium yellow light
   Pewter feet (not on pattern) yellow ocher, titanium white, burnt umber

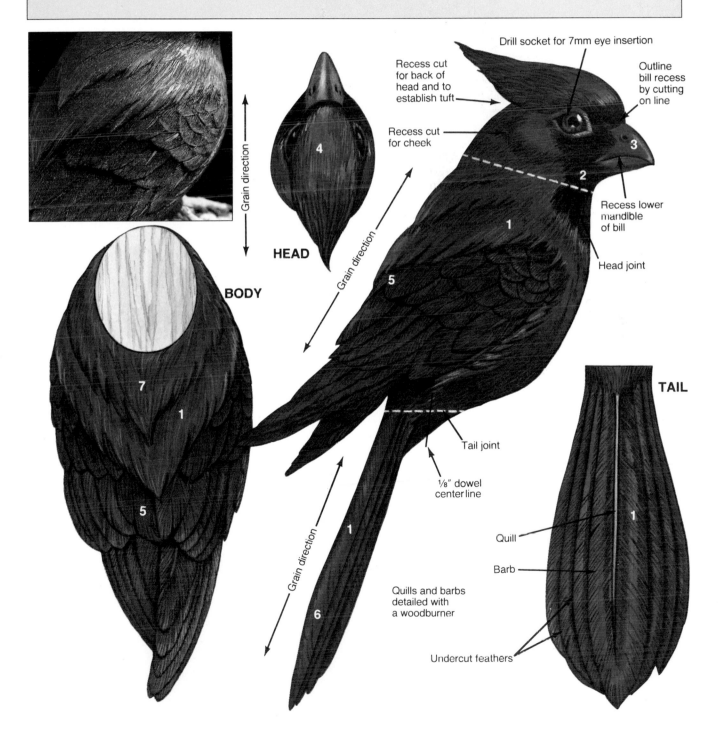

Grain direction

HEAD

Grain direction

BODY

Grain direction

Drill socket for 7mm eye insertion

Recess cut for back of head and to establish tuft

Recess cut for cheek

Outline bill recess by cutting on line

Recess lower mandible of bill

Head joint

Tail joint

⅛" dowel center line

Quills and barbs detailed with a woodburner

TAIL

Quill

Barb

Undercut feathers

CATCH A BLUEGILL

Racing, Wisconsin, carver Rick Beyer has fished since he was a kid. Today, though, he hardly finds time because he's busy carving award-winning fish. Cherry and a natural finish trademark Rick's work. But it's not just cherry's striking color that wins him top honors. "It's important to portray as much action as possible," he says.

Getting started in cherry

Rick carves cherry with power-carving equipment, such as a Dremel Moto-Tool. With only hand-carving tools, opt for softer stock, such as basswood.

For a fish à la Rick Beyer, you'll need a solid block of cherry measuring 6"x9" and a full 2½" thick. "Pick wood with straight grain running the length and no large, dark sap pockets," Rick advises. (Or start from a blank; see the Buying Guide *below right*.)

Trace the side view on the wood, then bandsaw the fish to shape. Next, stand the block up and draw on the top view. Saw along these lines.

To remove the extra wood along the back and bottom fins, around the head, and along the lower stomach, tilt your bandsaw table about 45° and follow the outline of the sawed-out blank. Now, carve the fins until you reach a ³⁄₁₆" thickness. Then, after referring to the cross section shown in the pattern, shape the body.

Next, sketch in an elongated, S-shaped curve on the tail fin. Place the body in a padded vise and remove the wood on the tail down to ³⁄₁₆" of thickness for final detailing.

Now you can start on the details—gills, eyes, and lips. Then, sand the fish's body and fins, tapering an edge on all body fins.

Featuring the fins

Pencil in and carve the ridges on the dorsal, lower, and tail fins. Cut the ventral and pectoral fins from scrap cherry with the grain running in the same direction as the fin ridges. Leave fins about ⅜" thick so you can add movement.

Next, hold the ventral and pectoral fins to the body and draw their base outline where they attach. Carve a slot for each fin at the angle you wish it to protrude. Trim the fins to fit. Finish-sand the body, then glue in the fins.

Find the location of the double nostrils (about ³⁄₁₆" away and down from each eye). Drill them with a ¹⁄₃₂" bit.

For a finish, Rick uses Formby's gloss tung oil. He sands between coats for smoothness.

Buying Guide
• **Cherry blank and fins.** For current prices, contact Beyer Galleries, 1115 N. Main, Racine, WI 53402.

Project Tool List
Bandsaw
Rotary power-carver
Ruby points for detailing
Kutzall bits for shaping

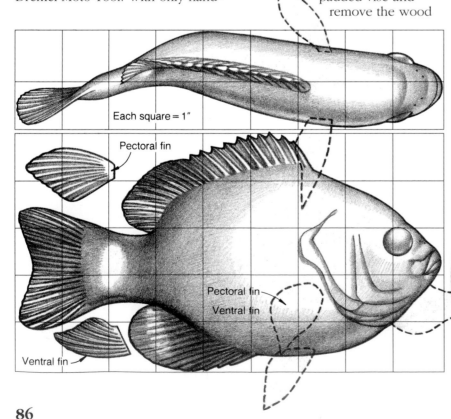

Each square = 1"

Pectoral fin

Pectoral fin
Ventral fin

Ventral fin

CRAFT A CALIFORNIA WHALE

Craftsman Bruce Stamp has always loved to work wood. As a kid, he built boats. One time, to his mother's dismay, Bruce "borrowed" a leaf from the family dining table to rework into a transom for a rowboat!

Now, Bruce pours his talent into re-creating in wood the shorebirds and marine life around California's Morrow Bay, where he lives and works. For feathers and flesh, Bruce substitutes eye-catching, exotic woods in many hues.

"I like to use mozambique for my sperm whales, but any dark wood will do," Bruce notes. "Whatever wood you select, you'll need a block of it measuring 2½x3x9". Although he mounts his sculptures on manzanita root, driftwood or a more traditional base will work.

Carving and finishing the sperm whale

"Lay out the pattern's top view on the 3" side of the wood, and

the side view on the 2½" side," Bruce says. "Then, bandsaw the top view from the nose to the tail, but not all the way through the tail end," he advises. "Next, do the same to the other side. This leaves the block with some support for sawing the side view." Then, turn the block on its side and finish

sawing the body.

Instead of hand carving, Bruce sculpts his creatures on a 1x42" strip sander with the table and platen removed. First, he contours the wood with a 50-grit belt, then refines with 150-, 240-, and 320-grit belts. Carving the whale's body, then sanding it, will give you the same result.

Drill a ⅛"-diameter eye hole about ⅛" deep on each side of the body, then make the fins. Bruce cuts his ⅛"-thick fins from scrap left from the body, and gently thins and tapers their edges. "To attach each one, I use a ⅜" length of wire, about the diameter of a brad, as a pin. I insert it in the body end of the fin," he says, "then drill holes and epoxy them in place." Drops of epoxy also will serve as the eyes, with dots of black paint for pupils. Complete your whale with any clear finish.

Project Tool List
Bandsaw
Strip sander
Portable drill

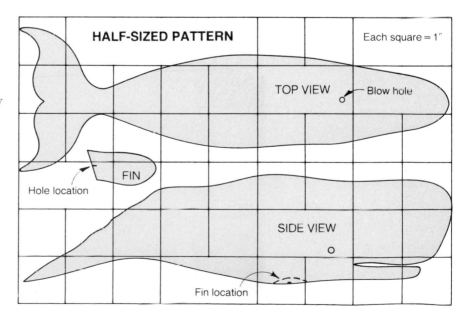

HALF-SIZED PATTERN

Each square = 1"

TOP VIEW — Blow hole

FIN

Hole location

SIDE VIEW

Fin location

A SERVING BOARD WITH STYLE

Else Bigton and her husband, Phil Odden, live amidst the timber surrounding Barronett, Wisconsin. In their Norsk Woodworks, they build and carve Scandinavian-style furniture.

Else trained to become a professional woodcarver in her native Norway. There, decoratively carved wooden serving pieces and utensils continue to be widely used. According to Else, the stylized dragon symbolized power and was a commonly featured motif during the Middle Ages.

True to Scandinavian tradition, Else selected birch for her project. "Scandinavian carvers prefer lighter-colored woods. Birch is also food-safe and hard enough to stand up as a cutting board on the noncarved side," she explains.

Tips on carving the dragon board

Enlarge the half-size pattern, then trace it onto a ¾x8½x17" birch board. Saw the board to shape and drill the ½" hole.

Else uses a V-tool to carve low-relief designs such as this. A chip carving knife will work, too.

To maintain the light, natural wood color, Else doesn't use a stain. Instead, she prefers a clear, nontoxic oil, such as Behlen's Salad Bowl Finish. Hang the finished board as a usable accent in your kitchen, den, or family room.

Project Tool List
Bandsaw
Gouges
   ⅜" No. 5
   ⅜" No. 6
   ½" No. 7
V-Tool, ³⁄₁₆" or ¼"
Chip-carving knife

½ SIZE

Each square = ½"

CARVE A SANTA

When Ron Ransom **first picked up a carving knife 11 years ago, he had no idea what it would lead to. "I carved plaques in relief, then shore- and songbirds, and even tried a duck decoy or two," recalls Ron. "Then, a couple of years back, I carved a Santa for my wife, Evelyn. While I was at it, I made a few more and took them to a craft show. Holy cow, they all sold!" Since then, the Marietta, Georgia, carver has focused on what he calls "Old World Santas." And, now he has dozens of designs.**

Getting Santa started

For Ron's Santa, you'll need a piece of basswood measuring 2x4¾x7¼" and a carving knife. Transfer the outline from the pattern onto the wood and bandsaw the figure to shape. Then, begin rounding the edges.

Next, draw in the lines for the face, hands, goose, and other details on the front. (The nearly flat back has only the continuation of the coat's trim and grooves separating the arms from the body.)

Now, start making stop cuts about ⅛" deep along the lines you drew. Then, lay your blade against the wood and cut to the lines.

Avoiding a break

"My Santas don't always have roly-poly faces," Ron comments, "but the features are rounded. The challenge is avoiding a square face." For definition, cut a line at least ¹⁄₁₆" deep to separate the cheeks and nose from the beard.

"For each eye, just leave a rounded area of wood the size of a pinhead," Ron advises, "then highlight them later with paint. For his beard, cut a series of grooves to varying depths."

Because the grain in your figure runs vertically, the carver cautions against accidentally breaking off the goose's head. "Don't try to carve its neck round and slender," Ron says. "Leave it a little wide."

Now, add the look of ages

Ron never sands the wood, but goes right to the painting. For this Santa, Ron applied acrylic paints in black, white, flesh, red, brown, and a metallic gold.

To give his Santas the antique look, Ron coats the painted figure with Griffin dark brown paste shoe polish ("Other brands give a purple tint"). He buffs the dry polish with a soft shoe brush, then lightens the fur and face by rubbing with neutral shoe polish. Enough brown will remain to give Santa a patina.

Project Tool List
Bandsaw
Carving knife

Each square = 1″

Enlarge at approx. 200% on copier, (twice at 141%)

IT'S A WESTERN SANTA

Now, trace the nose, mouth, and hat lines onto your head blank. Measure from the centerline to keep Santa symmetrical.

Carve Santa's body first

Note: *Treat Santa as two separate carvings. First, rough out his body, and then carve the details.*

Stop-cut the body pattern lines to begin carving Santa. Stopcuts, vertical knife cuts, enable you to carve to a line without chipping out the wood beyond it. As you form the body, leg, and arm contours with the ½" No. 3 and No. 9 gouges, make new stop cuts as needed. Leave the suspenders alone, for now.

Start the openings between the arms and the body by boring a hole with the ⅛" No. 11 gouge, twisting and pushing the tool. Begin the hole close to the body on the front, and angle it downward and inward as you bore through, coming out between Santa's back and arm. (See photo, *below.*)

Redraw the body centerline, and draw centerlines on the front and back of the boots, legs, and arms. Now, you're ready to start detailing Santa's body.

You say Santa Claus stays at the North Pole year-round? **Wrong! Arizona woodcarver Dave Rushlo spotted Claus in his cowboy clothes down in Scottsdale not too long ago. (At least, he *thinks* it was Santa.) Anyhow, Dave picked up his trusty knife and gouges and carved the old gent's likeness. If you too would like to have Western Santa around your home this season, gather your tools and have yourself a jolly old time carving this character.**

Bandsaw your blanks, and draw the guidelines

Transfer the full-sized patterns for Santa's body and head on *page 93* to your carving blocks. Arrange the body patterns so the boot soles rest on the same plane. Bandsaw the head and body blanks on the *yellow* lines, and then draw a vertical centerline around each as shown. Next, draw Santa's arms, legs, boots, belt, and suspenders on the body blank, as indicated by *pink* lines on the patterns. Referring to the Bottom View drawing, draw the boot soles on the bottom.

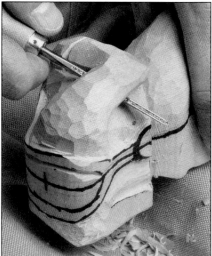

Bore through with your No. 11 gouge between the arm and body.

Detailing from the ground up

Let's start with those fancy boots Santa wears, shown in the opening photo. Cut the boot top, form the heels, and lay out the sole with a small V-tool. Now, shape the boot with your knife. Apply other details such as the pull straps, toe caps, and seams with the knife and small V-tool.

Next, carve the wrinkles and creases in Santa's jeans. Note in the photo how the fabric bunches up where he stuffs his jeans into his boots, and carve a slight rolled ridge around each boot top. Then, with a gouge or with rolling, sideways knife slices, carve folds and wrinkles on the ridge and legs. Add seams and front pockets with your V-tool.

Draw the rear pockets, belt, buckle, and belt loops with a pencil. Outline them with a small V-tool, and then carve. (Super-detailers note: Western Santa carries his chaw can in his right hip pocket.) When carving the belt, start with the buckle and belt loops; carve the belt last.

Upper-body exercises

Carve the arms, chest, and back to shape, enlarging the opening between Santa's arms and body. Refine the body contours, but leave the suspenders standing above the surface for now.

Shape a mitt on the end of each arm. Divide each mitt in half, and each half in half to form the fingers. Shorten the first and little fingers and carve them slightly lower than the two middle ones.

Carve each thumb up to the suspender, and then pare down the suspender at each hand so that it appears to go over the thumb and under the fingers (see photo, *above right*). Form the slightest hint of a thumb tip on the inside of each strap.

Draw fingernails with a pencil, and carve them, along with creases at the knuckles, with the small V-tool and knife. Santa wears a traditional red flannel garment with his jeans, so put a ribbed cuff at each wrist.

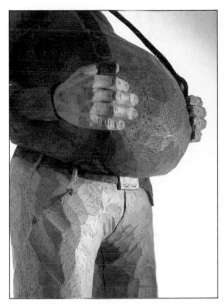

Roll the suspenders over Santa's thumbs, but take care not to hide his thumb tip.

Don't forget Santa's suspenders, whatever you do

You've pretty well finished Santa's body now, except for his suspenders. For those, you have a choice of two styles.

Undercut suspenders as shown in the photo, *below right,* really set off your carving. Before doing this type, though, reinforce them with cyanoacrylate adhesive (instant glue). Soak the wood with glue from shoulder to thumb, and let it dry for an hour.

Then, carefully dig out the wood under each strap from the thumb to the front of the shoulder. Cut a little bit at a time with your knife tip or small gouge.

For simpler suspenders, shave the wood to about 1/16" above the body surface. Straighten the edges with the small V-tool.

Completing the body

Now, draw a centered line across the shoulders on top the body. With a gouge and knife, bore a 1/2" neck hole about 1" deep where that line intersects the body centerline.

Carve a ribbed collar around the hole and add a couple of buttons on a placket at the front. Woodburn the boot and jean stitching along with boot-top and belt-buckle monograms.

Roughing Santa's head 'n' hat

Stop-cut the carving lines (*pink lines on pattern*) on the head with the 1/4" V-tool, and then carve the side of the face, hair, and beard to rough shape with the No. 3 gouge. Leave about 1/4" of extra material for the hair at the side of the face. Carve the neck peg to match the hole you made in Santa's body.

Remove side waste on the hat crown. Then, round the crown, using the front and back centerlines to maintain symmetry.

Lay out the brim on the top surface with the V-tool. Round the corners. Next, shave material from both sides with knife or gouges, forming a rolled brim about 1/8" thick. Carve the crown to shape, forming the creases.

Rough-in Santa's face

Refer to the head patterns, and draw the arcing line across the top of the nose, the circle at the end of the nose, and the contour on the side (*blue* pattern lines). Cut around the arcing line with the 1/4" V-tool, and carve the upper part of the nose to the contour line with knife and gouges.

Carve about 3/16" deep beside the nose and under the arc, and then cut in the eye sockets under the arc. Shape a ball on the end of the

continued

IT'S A WESTERN SANTA
continued

nose, following the circle you drew. Separate Santa's beard and mustache around the mouth, and then carve his lower lip with an arcing No. 11 gouge cut up into his mustache.

Start detailing at the top

Carve the furry ball on Santa's hat (see photo, *page 91*) and then, smooth out the crown and brim. Add a hatband, laying it out with your V-tool.

Undercut the top edge of the hatband slightly with your knife to make it stand out. Cut around the line under Santa's hat with your V-tool to make a crisp separation between hat and head.

His eyes, how they twinkle!

Refer to the close-up photo of Santa's face, on *page 94,* and then create eyebrows along the arcing line on each side of the nose with small V-tool cuts. Start Santa's eyes by drawing an arc in the top of each eye socket (for the fold in the upper lid) with another parallel arc about 1⁄16" lower (the eyelid itself). Draw the lower lid. Then, with a *sharp* V-tool, carve the fold line and the eyelid line.

Carve the eyeball with your knife, and then form the

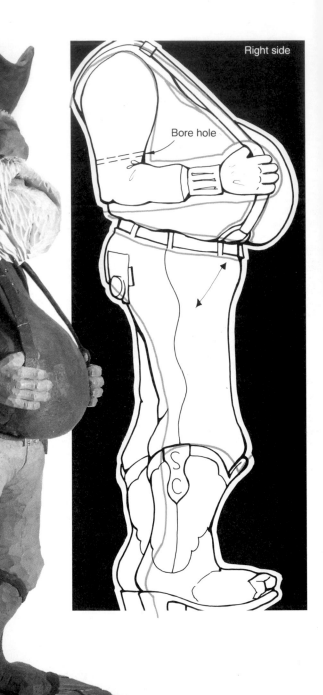

Right side

Bore hole

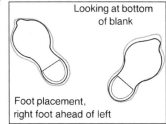

Looking at bottom of blank

Foot placement, right foot ahead of left

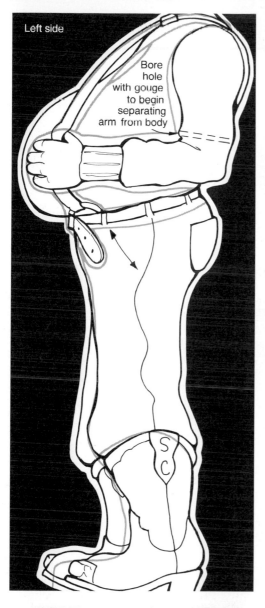

Left side

Bore hole with gouge to begin separating arm from body

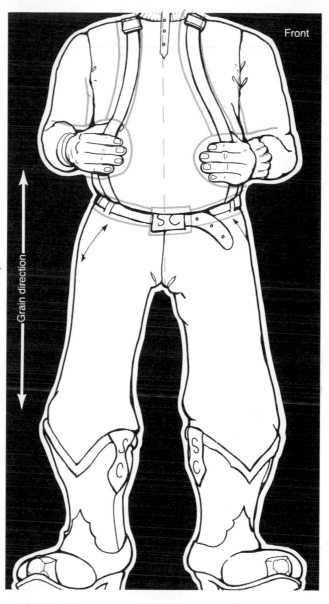

Front

Grain direction

Left side

FULL-SIZED CARVING BLANK PATTERNS

Cut on yellow lines to bandsaw carving blanks. Draw other lines as described in body of this article.

continued

IT'S A WESTERN SANTA
continued

lower lid with your V-tool. Santa is getting on in years and he smiles a lot, so add some crow's-feet at the corners of his eyes.

Smooth the cheeks and nose, paring the bridge of the nose down to blend it into the face. Add nostrils and open up Santa's mouth with the ⅛" No. 11 gouge. Draw flowing lines for Santa's hair, mustache, and beard, and carve them with short, curving gouge cuts. Then, go back with large and small V-tools for texture, again making short, curving cuts.

Build Santa a platform

Make the base from a piece of ¾" basswood about 7x9". Round the corners, as shown in the photographs, with your bandsaw. Undercut the edges for added interest.

With your V-tool, cut parallel straight lines about ½" apart lengthwise on the base. Simulate planked cabin flooring with random V-tool crosscuts. Texture the surface with a gouge, and then woodburn nailheads at the ends of each floorboard.

Carve Santa's bag from a 1½x3x4" block. Round the corners, and then represent rumpled fabric with deep V cuts. Add a gift list and a rope around the top. Stain the base walnut and the bag dark maple.

Paint your Santa

Painting is as important as the carving to the final effect. Thin the paints to a watery consistency— don't hide the character of your carving under heavy coats of paint. Build color by applying thin wash coats.

Santa's hair and beard and the ball on his hat get two coats of zinc white followed by two coats of titanium white. Paint the boots with golden ochre, and then add a coat of burnt umber on the bottom part. Trim the tops with Indian red.

Prime with zinc white before painting Santa's pants with cerulean blue and his red flannel top with Indian red. Hands and face get two coats of flesh hue followed by a coat of golden ochre.

After the paint dries, mount Santa and his bag on the base with 1¼" wood screws. Drill pilot holes, and then drive one screw into each of Santa's heels and one into the center of the bag from underneath the base. Countersink the screws. Finally, sign and date your masterpiece on the bottom of the base.

Supplies

Carving Stock: Basswood, jelutong, or other carving wood 3¼x2½x6" for the body and 2½x2½x3¾" for the head. Or, order a bandsawed basswood head and body. The two-piece set is available with guidelines drawn on, or without lines. For current prices, contact Dave Rushlo Woodcarvers Supply, 2530 N. 80th Pl., Scottsdale, AZ 85257. Suitable stock, ¾x7x9" for base and 1½x3x4" for bag. Knife: bench-type carving knife. Gouges: ⅛" and ½" No. 3, ¼" and ½" No. 9, ⅛" and ³⁄₁₆" No. 11; V-Tools: ⅛", ³⁄₁₆", and ¼" No. 41; Woodburner: fine-line tip, ¹⁄₁₆" circle tip; Finishing Materials: No. 8 and No. 12 shader brushes, No. 2 round brush, No. 00 or No. 000 liner brush; Artist's colors, oil or acrylic: titanium white, zinc white, black, golden ochre, burnt umber, Indian red, flesh hue, cerulean blue, and gold. Walnut and maple stain. If you use oil paints, you'll need thinner.

CARVE FATHER CHRISTMAS

"With this style," Harley explains, "a few lines and cuts can say a great deal."

At Christmas, Harley delves into his Scandinavian heritage to carve seasonal symbols. His favorite yuletide carving is Father Christmas. "Historically, the figure belongs to many Old World countries," he notes. "Father Christmas is not Santa Claus bearing gifts, but a spirit of love, goodwill, and caring."

The *WOOD*® magazine staff whittled Father Christmas at a workshop taught by Harley. The results were so pleasing we thought we'd share the pattern.

Carving and finishing Father Christmas

Harley carves air-dried northern basswood that he often harvests himself from the nearby wooded hills and valleys. This figure requires a 3x3x7" block of basswood or other paintable wood.

"The object is to carve the square block into a cylindrical shape," Harley says. "Pencil in a circular guideline on the base to follow. When you get to the arms, forget about roundness! The line from

elbow to coat cuff on each must be straight."

Texture the figure's beard and mustache with a narrow-angled V-tool. To give the fur trim a different look, switch to a small gouge.

Norma, Harley's wife, finishes his carvings. She thins acrylics to a wash consistency and brushes them on. "This method lets the wood-grain show through," explains Harley. "For a shadow effect, dip the colored figure in a mixture of boiled linseed oil and umber artist's oil color—about one teaspoon color to a quart of linseed oil. When it's dry, buff the carving with a wool sock for an old, well-handled look."

Buying Guide

• **Pre-sawn Blanks.** Father Christmas requires a 3x3x7" block of basswood on which to transfer the pattern shown *below left.* Or, start with a prime northern basswood blank sawn from two directions with lines drawn on to get you going. For current prices, contact Harley Refsal Woodcarving, 619 North St., Decorah, IA 52101.

Carver Harley Refsal makes his home in Decorah, Iowa, historic gateway for Scandinavian immigrant pioneers of the upper Midwest. Born in Minnesota of a Norwegian farm family, Harley knows firsthand the rural folk he likes to carve in caricature.

His rough-surfaced carving style lends itself well to the rough-hewn individuals who broke prairie ground. Harley calls the style "flat-plane" carving because it leaves the flat plane of each cut on the wood.

Each square = 1"

Project Tool List
Carving knife
³⁄₁₆" No. 5 gouge
V-Tool, ⅛"

ACKNOWLEDGMENTS

Writers

Wayne Barton—Decorative Carving, Swiss Style, pages 38–41

Larry Clayton—Hollow-Grind Sharpening, pages 20–25

Larry Johnston—Roughouts to the Rescue, 26–29; Decorative Carving, Swiss Style, pages 38–41; Carve a Colorful Feather Pin, pages 42–45; Making Faces, pages 48–51; Barkrosing, pages 52–53; Nature's Goodness Wall Plaque, pages 68–71

Bill Krier—How to Shop Smart for Carving Tools, pages 7–12; How to Sharpen Turning and Carving Tools, pages 13–18; Step-by-Step Relief Carving, pages 33–37

Harley J. Refsal— A Beginner's Guide to Basic Woodcarving Tools, pages 5–6; Making Faces, pages 48–51

Peter J. Stephano—The Wood that Carver's Crave, pages 30–31

Project Designers

James R. Barnett—Carve a Canvasback, pages 80–83

Rick Beyer—Carve a Bluegill, page 86

Elise Bigton—A Serving Board with Style, page 88

Desiree Hajny—Roscoe the Raccoon, pages 60–63; Here's Otto the Otter, pages 64–67

Harley J. Refsal—Tabletop Cigar-Store Indian, pages 72–75; The Norwegian Bachelor Farmer, pages 76–79; Carve Father Christmas, page 95

Harold Rosauer—Carve a Colorful Feather Pin, pages 42–45

Dave Rushlo—It's a Western Santa, pages 90–94

Bruce Stamp—Craft a California Whale, page 87

Robert Thomas Jr.—Carver's-Pride Trade Sign, pages 55–57

Bobbie Thurman—Carve Shalako: A Kachina-Style Pendant, page 58

Photographers

Harry Baumert
Brent Photography & Associates
Bob Calmer
Kay Danielson
Jim Elder
Jeff Frey
Bob Hawks
Darrell D. Henning
John Hetherington
William Hopkins
Hopkins Associates
Jim Kascoutas
Robert M. Miller
Bob Mischka
Chip Peterson
J. R. Raybourn
Perry Struse

Illustrators

Herb Dixon
Kim Downing
Desiree Hajny
Mike Henry
Norma Refsal
Jim Stevenson
Bill Zaun